350 FUN QUESTIONS
TO ENERGIZE YOUR RELATIONSHIP

THE COUPLE'S QUIZ BOOK

ALICIA MUÑOZ, LPC

ILLUSTRATIONS BY BETT NORRIS

ROCKRIDGE PRESS

To my son Lucas,
play master extraordinaire.

For general information on our other products and services or to obtain technical support, please contact our Customer Care Department within the United States at (866) 744-2665, or outside the United States at (510) 253-0500.

Rockridge Press publishes its books in a variety of electronic and print formats. Some content that appears in print may not be available in electronic books, and vice versa.

TRADEMARKS: Rockridge Press and the Rockridge Press logo are trademarks or registered trademarks of Callisto Media Inc. and/or its affiliates, in the United States and other countries, and may not be used without written permission. All other trademarks are the property of their respective owners. Rockridge Press is not associated with any product or vendor mentioned in this book.

Interior and Cover Designer: Angie Chiu
Art Producer: Hannah Dickerson
Editor: Anne Lowrey
Production Editor: Nora Milman

Illustrations © Bett Norris 2020
Author photo courtesy of © Tim Coburn

ISBN: Print 978-1-64611-765-9 | eBook 978-1-64611-766-6

R0

Contents

Introduction · vi

How to Use This Book · viii

PART ONE: US AS INDIVIDUALS · 1

CHAPTER ONE Favorite Things · 5

CHAPTER TWO Hobbies and Interests · 21

CHAPTER THREE Food · 37

CHAPTER FOUR Entertainment · 49

CHAPTER FIVE Personalities · 61

CHAPTER SIX Friends and Family · 77

CHAPTER SEVEN Travel · 89

PART TWO: US TOGETHER · 101

CHAPTER EIGHT Best Qualities · 105

CHAPTER NINE Intimacy · 115

CHAPTER TEN Our Past · 125

CHAPTER ELEVEN Our Present · 135

CHAPTER TWELVE Our Future · 145

CHAPTER THIRTEEN Our Couples Bucket List · 155

Bonus: Ask Me Anything · 159

References · 162

Introduction

Nothing fully prepares us for the unpredictable, high-octane, inspiring work of making the most of a romantic relationship. I say this with a great deal of certainty because long-term, committed love relationships are a personal and professional passion of mine. I'm not a romance novelist or a celebrity matchmaker: I'm a couples therapist. For more than 14 years, I've worked with countless couples at virtually every phase of their relationship journeys. And I've noticed two guiding principles that hold a particular kind of power in relationships:

1. Couples who play together, stay together.
2. Curiosity sustains intimacy.

Couples quizzes can draw on the generative potential of both of these principles, offering you and your partner a way to play while remaining curious. Pop quizzes may have caused anxiety in school, but when willingly and collaboratively engaged in, a quiz can also be a pleasurable "mind game" that sparks deeper conversations, insights, and sometimes even memorable make-out sessions on a living room couch (hey, you never know). Television producer Chuck Barris clearly recognized this in 1966, when *The Newlywed Game* became a syndicated hit. In the show, three or four couples compete against one another to see who *really* knows their partner.

Each member of a couple answers a series of questions in front of an audience—without the other partner listening—and the couple with the most in-sync responses wins.

Let me be clear: Competition is *not* the purpose of these quizzes. You won't be encouraged to "beat" your partner or any other couple (though a certain amount of playful competition can be a vitalizing energy throughout this process). Competition between partners is a bit like red wine or dark humor—a little may be okay, but too much is a buzzkill.

This book has been divided into two parts. In part 1, "Us as Individuals," the focus is on each of you separately. The quizzes shine a spotlight on your likes and dislikes across different domains, such as hobbies, interests, food, entertainment, and personality. In part 2, "Us Together," the quizzes incorporate your similarities and differences, focusing on your relationship and on you *as a couple*. Here, you'll work more collaboratively.

In each part, the subject matter combines light and playful themes and topics with complex and challenging ones. Of course, what's "light" or "heavy" and "simple" or "complex" is subjective. There's no universally "hard" or "easy" question or choice in these quizzes. Their significance will differ for everyone, and the answers will vary from one couple to the next.

How to Use This Book

Psychologist, researcher, and well-known couples therapist John Gottman says couples who are successful in their relationships "are well-versed in each other's likes, dislikes, personality quirks, hopes, and dreams." Many couples drift apart not because they have ill will toward one another or because their love vanishes but because other priorities have slowly supplanted their bond, like overgrown weeds in a neglected garden. Couples forget to be curious, ask questions, play together, and make time to understand and express feelings about one another's changing tastes and interests. Busyness overshadows a couple's natural curiosity and sense of fun, which can leave couples feeling emotionally distant even when physically close. Whether you're social distancing together or living parallel lives, couples quizzes are a handy way to connect or reconnect.

In part 1, you'll be making educated guesses about one another and learning more about your partner as a distinct, separate individual. For our purposes, the first person to do a chapter quiz is Partner A and the partner who follows is Partner B. The part 1 quizzes will repeat the same text back-to-back, allowing each partner to participate independently. At the end of each chapter in part 1, you can verify your answers with one another, marking your partner's responses with a check mark for "you got it" or an

"X" for "nice try but not quite." To avoid spoiling your fun with unnecessary conflict, pay attention to *how* you offer up your "correct" answers. Do this gracefully, saying, for example, "I appreciate how you responded to this one, and my answer is . . ." or "Good try, and I can see why you'd guess that. Do you want to hear my answer?" If you'd like some tips on asking and answering questions productively, skip ahead to the "Ask Me Anything" section on page 159.

After you've both completed the same quiz, you'll tally up your correct responses and write that number in the appropriate box under Partner A or Partner B. The person with the highest score for the most quizzes in each chapter wins the Quiz Master Prize, a reward designed to connect you and your partner through a pleasurable activity centered around each chapter's theme. These "prizes" are actually playful experiments to help you move out of thinking and into action. You can also come up with prizes of your own—or skip the "You've Earned It" section entirely.

You might consider jotting down thoughts, ideas, or insights that arise as you work through these quizzes. At the end of the book, in the "Ask Me Anything" section, you'll have an opportunity to revisit your notes and use them as starting points for creating some unique quizzes of your own.

PART ONE

Us as Individuals

Even if you've been together for 60 years, you still may not know the precise Halloween candy your partner treasured most as a kid, the average number of selfies they take per week, or an alternate name they might have wished to have been given at birth. But don't sweat it—by the end of part 1, you'll know all this and more. Whether you're a couple and have spent decades together or you've been together a short while, it doesn't change the fact that you are separate individuals with your own thoughts, hopes, and challenges your partner may not know. These quizzes will give you many chances to learn a lot more about each other.

Each quiz in part 1 appears twice. Partner A reads and answers their copy of the quiz first and then passes the book to Partner B, who reads and answers their copy of the same quiz. Once you've both completed the quizzes in a chapter, you can go over one another's answers, take in what you've learned, and tally up your points. Unless otherwise indicated, each quiz question is worth one point.

Every chapter will close with a "Replay" section reviewing the chapter's theme followed by a "You've Earned It" section, in which the person with the most points—the higher scorer for that chapter's quizzes—claims their Quiz Master Prize. This section applies if you've both agreed to play for prizes but is optional. The Quiz Master Prizes are designed as "win-wins," drawing from your answers to the quizzes themselves, so there's no need to fret if your partner gets more "right" answers than you do. These end-of-chapter rewards will help you put the book's different themes into action as you practice the essential couples' skills of giving and receiving.

Be aware of any unconscious temptation to prove you're "better" at the who-knows-who-more game or to "win" for any reason other than the cheerful frisson generated by friendly competition. The purpose of this book is to bring you closer, not to leave either of you boasting a lonely victory.

CHAPTER ONE

Favorite Things

It's a psychological truth that the things we like—our favorite things—reflect who we are and also play a part in *shaping* who we are. Whether material or immaterial, our favorite things distinguish us from others around us. They're clues to our pasts, symptoms of our needs and priorities, and reflections of our personalities. Our favorite things are like golden threads woven through the fabric of our identity—connecting our values, attitudes, style, and experience of the world. Knowing—and getting to know—your partner's "favorite things" is one way of supporting them, seeing them, and helping them feel at home in your relationship.

Quiz 1: Little Things

1. Describe your partner's favorite type of pillow.
    a. Down
    b. Memory foam
    c. Polyester
    d. Microbead
    e. Buckwheat
    f. Contour
    g. Body

2. **(Circle one.)** Your partner would prefer a **nonalcoholic /
   alcoholic** drink to help them relax.

3. Your partner's favorite freebies are:
    a. Free phone apps
    b. Food samples
    c. Airline eye masks
    d. Hotel toiletries
    e. Other: _____

4. Your partner's favorite reading material falls into the
   category of:
    a. Fiction
    b. Autobiographies
    c. Self-help
    d. Internet news
    e. Other: _____

5. **(True/False)** Your partner likes to wear racy underclothing.

6. Your partner's favorite Halloween candy as a kid was:
   a. Candy corn
   b. Smarties
   c. Licorice
   d. M&M's
   e. Other: _____

7. List one "favorite thing" with sentimental value your partner likes to wear: _____

8. Your partner's most productive time of day is:
   a. Morning (5 a.m. to 11 a.m.)
   b. Afternoon (12 p.m. to 5 p.m.)
   c. Night (6 p.m. to 10 p.m.)
   d. Late night (11 p.m. to 4 a.m.)

9. **(True/False)** Your partner selects toilet paper rolls based on longevity over texture.

10. Your partner's favorite way to communicate is:
    a. Text
    b. E-mail
    c. Face-to-face
    d. Phone
    e. Video call/FaceTime
    f. Handwritten notes

PARTNER A TOTAL: _____

Quiz 1: Little Things

1. Describe your partner's favorite type of pillow.
    a. Down
    b. Memory foam
    c. Polyester
    d. Microbead
    e. Buckwheat
    f. Contour
    g. Body

2. **(Circle one.)** Your partner would prefer a **nonalcoholic** / **alcoholic** drink to help them relax.

3. Your partner's favorite freebies are:
    a. Free phone apps
    b. Food samples
    c. Airline eye masks
    d. Hotel toiletries
    e. Other: _____

4. Your partner's favorite reading material falls into the category of:
    a. Fiction
    b. Autobiographies
    c. Self-help
    d. Internet news
    e. Other: _____

5. **(True/False)** Your partner likes to wear racy underclothing.

6. Your partner's favorite Halloween candy as a kid was:
    a. Candy corn
    b. Smarties
    c. Licorice
    d. M&M's
    e. Other: _____

7. List one "favorite thing" with sentimental value your partner likes to wear: _____

8. Your partner's most productive time of day is:
    a. Morning (5 a.m. to 11 a.m.)
    b. Afternoon (12 p.m. to 5 p.m.)
    c. Night (6 p.m. to 10 p.m.)
    d. Late night (11 p.m. to 4 a.m.)

9. **(True/False)** Your partner selects toilet paper rolls based on longevity over texture.

10. Your partner's favorite way to communicate is:
    a. Text
    b. E-mail
    c. Face-to-face
    d. Phone
    e. Video call/FaceTime
    f. Handwritten notes

PARTNER B TOTAL: _____

Quiz 2: Big Things

1. If your partner owned a mansion, they'd spend most of their time in the:
   a. State-of-the-art kitchen
   b. Multilevel luxury garage
   c. Swimming pool
   d. Greenhouse
   e. Other: _____

2. If your partner was selected to orchestrate a new, nationally televised, competitive sporting event, it would most likely involve _____.

3. Your partner's favorite part of the country is the:
   a. Northeast
   b. Midwest
   c. South
   d. West

4. **(True/False)** Your partner plans to work in retirement.

5. Your partner's favorite vacation location is:
   a. On a beach
   b. On a boat/cruise ship
   c. In the mountains
   d. At home on the couch
   e. At an animal sanctuary
   f. In a major city
   g. In a jungle

6. The thought leader or expert whose ideas your partner currently most admires is _____.

7. Circle the three terms that best describe the architectural style your partner favors:

Modern	Mid-century modern
Historic	Victorian
Floor-to-ceiling windows	Minimalist
Multiple floors	American craftsman
Ranch	Farmhouse
Colonial	Brownstone

8. Your partner's favorite job would be best described as:
   a. What they do now
   b. Service-related
   c. High risk/high thrill
   d. Creative
   e. Technology-related
   f. Advocacy work

9. **(Circle one.)** Would your partner rather attain wealth **effortlessly** (e.g., lottery, inheritance) or through **hard work**?

10. The pattern your partner feels most drawn to is:
    a. Tartan
    b. Argyle
    c. Houndstooth
    d. Paisley
    e. Polka dots
    f. Stripes

PARTNER A TOTAL: _____

Quiz 2: Big Things

1. If your partner owned a mansion, they'd spend most of their time in the:
    a. State-of-the-art kitchen
    b. Multilevel luxury garage
    c. Swimming pool
    d. Greenhouse
    e. Other: _____

2. If your partner was selected to orchestrate a new, nationally televised, competitive sporting event, it would most likely involve _____.

3. Your partner's favorite part of the country is the:
    a. Northeast
    b. Midwest
    c. South
    d. West

4. **(True/False)** Your partner plans to work in retirement.

5. Your partner's favorite vacation location is:
    a. On a beach
    b. On a boat/cruise ship
    c. In the mountains
    d. At home on the couch
    e. At an animal sanctuary
    f. In a major city
    g. In a jungle

6. The thought leader or expert whose ideas your partner currently most admires is _____.

7. Circle the three terms that best describe the architectural style your partner favors:

Modern	Mid-century modern
Historic	Victorian
Floor-to-ceiling windows	Minimalist
Multiple floors	American craftsman
Ranch	Farmhouse
Colonial	Brownstone

8. Your partner's favorite job would be best described as:
   a. What they do now
   b. Service-related
   c. High risk/high thrill
   d. Creative
   e. Technology-related
   f. Advocacy work

9. **(Circle one.)** Would your partner rather attain wealth **effortlessly** (e.g., lottery, inheritance) or through **hard work**?

10. The pattern your partner feels most drawn to is:
    a. Tartan
    b. Argyle
    c. Houndstooth
    d. Paisley
    e. Polka dots
    f. Stripes

PARTNER B TOTAL: _____

Quiz 3: Any Things

1. Your partner's favorite day of the week is:
   a. Friday
   b. Saturday
   c. Sunday
   d. Monday (they love their job)
   e. Tuesday
   f. Wednesday
   g. Thursday

2. A person of integrity your partner admires is

   _____.

3. Out of these five things, which would be your partner's favorite? (+1 bonus point if you can name the musical these song lyrics reference!)
   a. Crisp apple strudels
   b. Bright copper kettles and warm woolen mittens
   c. Wild geese that fly with the moon on their wings
   d. Silver-white winters that melt into springs
   e. Raindrops on roses

4. Your partner's go-to coffee shop drink is

   _____.

5. Your partner feels most loved when you:
   a. Give them attention and presence
   b. Give them a thoughtful gift or note

    c.   Hug them or show affection

    d.   Praise them

6. Your partner's favorite TED talk is by
   _____. If they don't watch
   TED talks, who would they like most to see speak in front
   of a crowd? _____

7. **(True/False)** In December, your partner hums along to
   holiday songs.

8. If your partner could bring their favorite deceased pet
   (or any fictional animal) to life, they'd choose

   _____.

9. Your partner's favorite way to socialize is:

       a.   With a group of friends

       b.   With you and one other couple

       c.   With just one other friend

       d.   With strangers (future friends)

10. Your partner's most common method to pay bills is:

        a.   Postal service/snail mail

        b.   Online

        c.   Desperately, after late fees hit

        d.   Transferring balance to lower-interest credit card

PARTNER A TOTAL: _____

Quiz 3: Any Things

1. Your partner's favorite day of the week is:
   a. Friday
   b. Saturday
   c. Sunday
   d. Monday (they love their job)
   e. Tuesday
   f. Wednesday
   g. Thursday

2. A person of integrity your partner admires is

   _____.

3. Out of these five things, which would be your partner's favorite? (+1 bonus point if you can name the musical these song lyrics reference!)
   a. Crisp apple strudels
   b. Bright copper kettles and warm woolen mittens
   c. Wild geese that fly with the moon on their wings
   d. Silver-white winters that melt into springs
   e. Raindrops on roses

4. Your partner's go-to coffee shop drink is

   _____.

5. Your partner feels most loved when you:
   a. Give them attention and presence
   b. Give them a thoughtful gift or note

    c.   Hug them or show affection

    d.   Praise them

6. Your partner's favorite TED talk is by

_____. If they don't watch
TED talks, who would they like most to see speak in front
of a crowd? _____

7. **(True/False)** In December, your partner hums along to
holiday songs.

8. If your partner could bring their favorite deceased pet
(or any fictional animal) to life, they'd choose

_____.

9. Your partner's favorite way to socialize is:

    a.   With a group of friends

    b.   With you and one other couple

    c.   With just one other friend

    d.   With strangers (future friends)

10. Your partner's most common method to pay bills is:

    a.   Postal service/snail mail

    b.   Online

    c.   Desperately, after late fees hit

    d.   Transferring balance to lower-interest credit card

PARTNER B TOTAL: _____

REPLAY

You've begun to give some serious thought to your partner's favorite things, from the type of pillow they like to their favorite way to socialize. Hopefully, you know your partner a little better than you did before this chapter and now see the shine of some new "golden threads" in their preferences, attitudes, and inclinations.

YOU'VE EARNED IT!

Quiz Master Prize: The person with the most points will choose a favorite TED talk, podcast, or audiobook chapter to listen to together. The other partner will focus on giving them love in the form of their answer to question 5 of quiz 3.

CHAPTER TWO

Hobbies and Interests

Our hobbies and interests are ways we continue to play in our adult lives. When we call painting or dancing a "hobby" or mountain climbing and baseball "interests," it adds purposefulness and acceptability to our pleasures in a world where, as adults, we're conditioned to focus on performance and productivity. Being curious about our partner's hobbies and interests helps us connect to the inner child that lives within them—and within us.

Even if you don't share your partner's interests and hobbies, knowing more about activities that inspire you both may give you an opportunity to expand what you take pleasure in and to include one another more in activities you tend to do alone. Often, couples find that despite differences, there's a space—as with a Venn diagram—where the ways they like to play overlap and can become integrated into their lives as partnered adults over time.

Quiz 1: Leisure Time

1. Your partner's preferred way of relaxing after a long workweek is _____.

2. Circle the most likely highlight of your partner's ideal beach vacation.
   a. Lounging under an umbrella
   b. Scuba diving
   c. Getting a massage or other spa service
   d. Ordering drinks by the pool
   e. Jet Skiing
   f. Other: _____

3. **(True/False)** Given the choice, your partner would prefer playing a competitive game over a collaborative one.

4. **(Circle all that apply.)** Which of these phrases capture your partner's associations with "leisure"?

Alone time	Good food
Unplugging from devices	A glass of wine/beer
Plugging into devices	Nature
Sharing experiences	Exercising
No responsibilities	Time with animals/kids

5. Which expression best encapsulates your partner's attitude toward hard work?
   a. Nobody on their deathbed said, "I wish I'd spent more time at the office."
   b. Those at the top of the mountain didn't fall there.

c. Work hard, play hard.

d. Genius is 1 percent inspiration, 99 percent perspiration.

6. Which of these leisure activities/hobbies has your partner *never* tried?

   a. Knitting   d. Horseback riding
   b. Waterskiing   e. Snorkeling
   c. Painting   f. Bird-watching

7. Does your partner believe in answering work calls/e-mails on the weekend?

   a. Never   c. Often
   b. In emergency situations   d. Always

8. If your partner could reorganize the workweek to suit their personal preferences, they would start work at ____, end work at ____, and work ____ days a week.

9. Rate these activities from 1 to 5 with one being "most" and 5 being "least" preferred by your partner.

   ____ Reading a book   ____ Going to a yoga class
   ____ Watching a movie   ____ Going out with friends
   ____ Listening to music

10. A leisure activity your partner could easily overindulge in is:

    a. Eating   d. Drinking alcohol
    b. Video/online games   e. Shopping
    c. Gambling   f. Sleeping

PARTNER A TOTAL: _____

Quiz 1: Leisure Time

1. Your partner's preferred way of relaxing after a long workweek is _____.

2. Circle the most likely highlight of your partner's ideal beach vacation.
    a. Lounging under an umbrella
    b. Scuba diving
    c. Getting a massage or other spa service
    d. Ordering drinks by the pool
    e. Jet Skiing
    f. Other: _____

3. **(True/False)** Given the choice, your partner would prefer playing a competitive game over a collaborative one.

4. **(Circle all that apply.)** Which of these phrases capture your partner's associations with "leisure"?

Alone time	Good food
Unplugging from devices	A glass of wine/beer
Plugging into devices	Nature
Sharing experiences	Exercising
No responsibilities	Time with animals/kids

5. Which expression best encapsulates your partner's attitude toward hard work?
    a. Nobody on their deathbed said, "I wish I'd spent more time at the office."
    b. Those at the top of the mountain didn't fall there.

c. Work hard, play hard.

d. Genius is 1 percent inspiration, 99 percent perspiration.

6. Which of these leisure activities/hobbies has your partner *never* tried?

a. Knitting

b. Waterskiing

c. Painting

d. Horseback riding

e. Snorkeling

f. Bird-watching

7. Does your partner believe in answering work calls/e-mails on the weekend?

a. Never

b. In emergency situations

c. Often

d. Always

8. If your partner could reorganize the workweek to suit their personal preferences, they would start work at ___, end work at ___, and work ___ days a week.

9. Rate these activities from 1 to 5 with one being "most" and 5 being "least" preferred by your partner.

___ Reading a book

___ Watching a movie

___ Listening to music

___ Going to a yoga class

___ Going out with friends

10. A leisure activity your partner could easily overindulge in is:

a. Eating

b. Video/online games

c. Gambling

d. Drinking alcohol

e. Shopping

f. Sleeping

PARTNER B TOTAL: _____

Quiz 2: Creative Minds

1. What creative activity has your partner engaged in most often this week?
   a. Drawing/painting
   b. Music-related (playing/listening)
   c. Reading
   d. Blogging/writing
   e. Graphic design
   f. Car repairs
   g. Acting/performing
   h. Other: _____

2. Your creative hobby or interest that benefits your partner most is:
   a. Cooking
   b. Home repair
   c. Landscaping/gardening
   d. Scrapbooking
   e. Exercising/staying fit
   f. Home decorating
   g. Party planning

3. **(True/False)** Your partner knows what a vision board is.

4. Looking back, if your partner could have learned to play a musical instrument early in life (or an additional instrument), it would have been the _____.

5. The interest your partner least enjoys sharing with you is:
   a. Going to an art gallery
   b. Activism
   c. Sudoku/crossword
   d. Hiking
   e. Other: _____

6. **(True/False)** Your partner can name at least one famous love poem along with the poet.

7. A creative interest your partner hopes you'll one day share with them is _____.

8. Which hobby excites your partner the most?
   a. Geocaching
   b. Stone skipping
   c. Stamp collecting
   d. Getting tattoos
   e. Other: _____

9. Out of the 206 bones in the human body, your partner has broken precisely _____ of them over the course of their life.

10. One creative interest your partner wishes they could use in their current job is _____.

PARTNER A TOTAL: _____

Quiz 2: Creative Minds

1. What creative activity has your partner engaged in most often this week?
   a. Drawing/painting
   b. Music-related (playing/listening)
   c. Reading
   d. Blogging/writing
   e. Graphic design
   f. Car repairs
   g. Acting/performing
   h. Other: _____

2. Your creative hobby or interest that benefits your partner most is:
   a. Cooking
   b. Home repair
   c. Landscaping/gardening
   d. Scrapbooking
   e. Exercising/staying fit
   f. Home decorating
   g. Party planning

3. **(True/False)** Your partner knows what a vision board is.

4. Looking back, if your partner could have learned to play a musical instrument early in life (or an additional instrument), it would have been the _____.

5. The interest your partner least enjoys sharing with you is:
   a. Going to an art gallery
   b. Activism
   c. Sudoku/crossword
   d. Hiking
   e. Other: _____

6. **(True/False)** Your partner can name at least one famous love poem along with the poet.

7. A creative interest your partner hopes you'll one day share with them is _____.

8. Which hobby excites your partner the most?
   a. Geocaching
   b. Stone skipping
   c. Stamp collecting
   d. Getting tattoos
   e. Other: _____

9. Out of the 206 bones in the human body, your partner has broken precisely _____ of them over the course of their life.

10. One creative interest your partner wishes they could use in their current job is _____.

PARTNER B TOTAL: _____

Quiz 3: Adrenaline Rushes

1. **(True/False)** Your partner prefers hobbies and interests that spike their adrenaline over ones that are peaceful, creative, or meditative.

2. When your partner is excited about a hobby or interest, they:
   - a. Vibrate with energy
   - b. Talk really fast
   - c. Turn into a drill sergeant
   - d. Giggle a lot
   - e. Other: _____

3. Which of these hobbies do you think your partner would pursue if it wasn't risky?
   - a. Rock climbing
   - b. Parasailing
   - c. Scuba diving
   - d. Jet Skiing
   - e. Dirt biking
   - f. Skateboarding
   - g. Other: _____

4. Your partner likes exercising most:
   - a. In a group of people
   - b. With a trainer
   - c. Competitively on a team
   - d. Competitively solo

5. Your partner's closest near-death experience took place (or is most likely to take place) pursuing the following interest/hobby:
   - a. Eating at a new restaurant
   - b. Trying out a new gizmo or gadget

    c.   Zip-lining

    d.   White-water rafting

    e.   Forgetting to stay hydrated while writing

    f.   Feeding hungry pigeons

    g.   Other: _____

6. **(Circle all that apply.)** Your partner has *never* considered developing the following interest/hobby:

    Bungee jumping

    Wing walking

    Knife juggling

    Fire department volunteering

7. **(True/False)** Zorbing is on your partner's bucket list—or would be if they knew what it was. (+1 bonus point if you can explain what zorbing is to your partner!)

8. The hill or park where your partner went sledding or played as a kid was _____.

9. A cold-weather activity your partner wants to do more of is:

    a.   Ice hockey   d.   Snowmobiling

    b.   Downhill skiing   e.   All of the above

    c.   Ice-skating   f.   None of the above

10. **(Circle one.)** Your partner is the **helmet-wearing type** / **non-helmet-wearing type**.

PARTNER A TOTAL: _____

Quiz 3: Adrenaline Rushes

1. **(True/False)** Your partner prefers hobbies and interests that spike their adrenaline over ones that are peaceful, creative, or meditative.

2. When your partner is excited about a hobby or interest, they:
   - a. Vibrate with energy
   - b. Talk really fast
   - c. Turn into a drill sergeant
   - d. Giggle a lot
   - e. Other: _____

3. Which of these hobbies do you think your partner would pursue if it wasn't risky?
   - a. Rock climbing
   - b. Parasailing
   - c. Scuba diving
   - d. Jet Skiing
   - e. Dirt biking
   - f. Skateboarding
   - g. Other: _____

4. Your partner likes exercising most:
   - a. In a group of people
   - b. With a trainer
   - c. Competitively on a team
   - d. Competitively solo

5. Your partner's closest near-death experience took place (or is most likely to take place) pursuing the following interest/hobby:
   - a. Eating at a new restaurant
   - b. Trying out a new gizmo or gadget

<ol type="a" start="3">
<li>Zip-lining</li>
<li>White-water rafting</li>
<li>Forgetting to stay hydrated while writing</li>
<li>Feeding hungry pigeons</li>
<li>Other: _____</li>
</ol>

6. **(Circle all that apply.)** Your partner has *never* considered developing the following interest/hobby:

    Bungee jumping

    Wing walking

    Knife juggling

    Fire department volunteering

7. **(True/False)** Zorbing is on your partner's bucket list—or would be if they knew what it was. (+1 bonus point if you can explain what zorbing is to your partner!)

8. The hill or park where your partner went sledding or played as a kid was _____.

9. A cold-weather activity your partner wants to do more of is:

<table>
<tr><td>a. Ice hockey</td><td>d. Snowmobiling</td></tr>
<tr><td>b. Downhill skiing</td><td>e. All of the above</td></tr>
<tr><td>c. Ice-skating</td><td>f. None of the above</td></tr>
</table>

10. **(Circle one.)** Your partner is the **helmet-wearing type / non-helmet-wearing type**.

    PARTNER B TOTAL: _____

REPLAY

By now, you likely have a clearer sense of the types of hobbies your partner enjoys and whether they gravitate toward activities that are creative, relaxing, or intense. Maybe you've learned something new about your partner's interests or you've found common ground in what thrills, inspires, and excites both of you. Use this new information to step out of your comfort zones and explore your hobbies and interests together.

YOU'VE EARNED IT!

Quiz Master Prize: Your partner participates in the hobby or interest of your choice. Let them know how you'd like them to join you in a specific activity. For example: "Come to a baseball game with me and root for my team," "Be my *sous-chef* as I cook us a meal," or "Come to the gym and join me in a workout."

CHAPTER THREE
Food

It can be tempting to overlook the significance of food in a romantic relationship, particularly if you have easy access to good food. Yet there's no denying that the way we share and exchange food with a partner speaks volumes about our intimacy.

In addition, our opinions on cooking, grocery shopping, processed foods, leftovers, and nutrition weave their way into how we nurture ourselves and others. The truism "you are what you eat" may be an oversimplification, but there's no denying that our choices—conscious and unconscious—related to nutrition impact our health, energy levels, and mood and, by extension, the quality of our closest relationships.

In these quizzes, you'll be asked about your partner's attitude toward food as well as specifics and details—from their point of view—related to cooking, eating out, health food, junk food, and more.

Quiz 1: Food for Thought

1. Your partner likes it most when you:
    a. Don't touch their food
    b. Accept their food when they offer it
    c. Encourage them to take food from your plate
    d. Let them feed you
    e. Feed them

2. **(True/False)** Your partner made their own school lunches as a kid.

3. Your partner thinks of their family meals as times of:
    a. Friendly chaos
    b. Rigid rules related to etiquette
    c. Stimulating conversations
    d. Quiet desperation
    e. Open conflict
    f. Other: _____

4. If nutrition didn't matter, the food your partner would eat most in a day is _____.

5. **(True/False)** Your partner harbors a secret wish to watch you cook naked.

6. Your partner would describe themselves as a(n):
    a. Omnivore
    b. Carnivore
    c. Vegan

   d.   Vegetarian

   e.   Pescatarian

   f.   Other: _____

7. **(True/False)** Sometimes your partner gives quiet thanks for their food.

8. Select a phrase from each column that comes closest to describing your partner's default eating style:

Big biter	Small biter
Quick chewer	Slow chewer
Wolfs food down	Eats like a bird
Talks while chewing	Mindful eater

9. One psychological need that food satisfies for your partner is:

   a.   Love

   b.   Safety

   c.   Numbing out

   d.   Control

   e.   Comfort

10. If your partner could hybridize two fruits or vegetables, they'd create a cross between a _____ and a _____.

PARTNER A TOTAL: _____

Quiz 1: Food for Thought

1. Your partner likes it most when you:
    a. Don't touch their food
    b. Accept their food when they offer it
    c. Encourage them to take food from your plate
    d. Let them feed you
    e. Feed them

2. **(True/False)** Your partner made their own school lunches as a kid.

3. Your partner thinks of their family meals as times of:
    a. Friendly chaos
    b. Rigid rules related to etiquette
    c. Stimulating conversations
    d. Quiet desperation
    e. Open conflict
    f. Other: _____

4. If nutrition didn't matter, the food your partner would eat most in a day is _____.

5. **(True/False)** Your partner harbors a secret wish to watch you cook naked.

6. Your partner would describe themselves as a(n):
    a. Omnivore
    b. Carnivore
    c. Vegan

    d. Vegetarian

    e. Pescatarian

    f. Other: _____

7. **(True/False)** Sometimes your partner gives quiet thanks for their food.

8. Select a phrase from each column that comes closest to describing your partner's default eating style:

Big biter	Small biter
Quick chewer	Slow chewer
Wolfs food down	Eats like a bird
Talks while chewing	Mindful eater

9. One psychological need that food satisfies for your partner is:

    a. Love

    b. Safety

    c. Numbing out

    d. Control

    e. Comfort

B

10. If your partner could hybridize two fruits or vegetables, they'd create a cross between a _____ and a _____.

PARTNER B TOTAL: _____

Quiz 2: Eating Out, Eating In

1. If your partner is hungry and the refrigerator is empty, they'll most likely:
    a. Order pizza
    b. Order Chinese food
    c. Pick up something premade from a deli
    d. Buy ingredients and cook from scratch
    e. Go hungry

2. **(True/False)** Generally, your partner loves dining out.

3. Circle the words your partner associates with "home-cooked meal."

Delicious	Culinary delight
Bland	TV dinner
What's that?	Dad
Overdone	Gourmet
Cold	Mac and cheese
Stressful	Mom

4. One restaurant where your partner wants to take you is _____.

5. Your partner's dream breakfast in bed would *not* include:
    a. Avocado toast
    b. Smoked salmon
    c. Breakfast tacos
    d. Fish eggs
    e. Sausage or bacon
    f. Milk or yogurt
    g. Orange juice
    h. Granola

6. A meal your partner prepared regularly for themself as a kid was _____.

7. Your partner's ideal dinner out begins with:
   a. Bread and butter
   b. A salad
   c. A bowl of soup
   d. Crackers and cheese
   e. An amuse-bouche (+1 bonus point if you know what this French phrase means!)
   f. A special drink

8. **(Circle one.)** The person who wants to go out to dinner most in your relationship is **you** / **your partner**.

9. Your partner has ordered takeout (including room service) roughly ____ times in the past month.

10. The ideal next meal your partner would love to have today is _____.

PARTNER A TOTAL: _____

Quiz 2: Eating Out, Eating In

1. If your partner is hungry and the refrigerator is empty, they'll most likely:
    a. Order pizza
    b. Order Chinese food
    c. Pick up something premade from a deli
    d. Buy ingredients and cook from scratch
    e. Go hungry

2. **(True/False)** Generally, your partner loves dining out.

3. Circle the words your partner associates with "home-cooked meal."

Delicious	Culinary delight
Bland	TV dinner
What's that?	Dad
Overdone	Gourmet
Cold	Mac and cheese
Stressful	Mom

4. One restaurant where your partner wants to take you is _____.

5. Your partner's dream breakfast in bed would *not* include:
    a. Avocado toast
    b. Smoked salmon
    c. Breakfast tacos
    d. Fish eggs
    e. Sausage or bacon
    f. Milk or yogurt
    g. Orange juice
    h. Granola

6. A meal your partner prepared regularly for themself
   as a kid was _____.

7. Your partner's ideal dinner out begins with:
   a. Bread and butter
   b. A salad
   c. A bowl of soup
   d. Crackers and cheese
   e. An amuse-bouche (+1 bonus point if you know
      what this French phrase means!)
   f. A special drink

8. **(Circle one.)** The person who wants to go out to dinner
   most in your relationship is **you** / **your partner**.

9. Your partner has ordered takeout (including room service)
   roughly ____ times in the past month.

10. The ideal next meal your partner would love to have
    today is _____.

PARTNER B TOTAL: _____

REPLAY

You've just completed quizzes with questions on whether your partner likes it when you take food from their plate, what psychological need food fulfills for them, and how many times your partner has ordered takeout in the last month. You know the fruits and/or vegetables your partner would hybridize, and you've even honed in on what your partner would like to eat next.

The more you understand about one another's food preferences and practices, along with your beliefs and opinions about home-cooked meals and eating out, the easier it will be to co-create more satisfying gastronomic experiences.

YOU'VE EARNED IT!

Quiz Master Prize: Invite your partner to the restaurant you want to take them to (question 4, quiz 2), or suggest an alternative venue where the two of you might be able to order at least one of your favorite desserts and celebrate your Quiz Master awesomeness together.

CHAPTER FOUR

Entertainment

Performances of all kinds—at the movies, on computer screens, onstage, or even on boardwalks in Key West—have the power to hold our rapt attention and delight us. Whether you like dance, theater, sports, the circus, movies, YouTube videos, TV shows, skateboarding competitions, or jazz ensembles, different forms of entertainment are woven into the fabric of our everyday lives, sometimes in ways that are central to our sense of self.

The forms of entertainment you and your partner enjoy say a lot about you as people—about your heritage, your upbringing, your comfort level with pleasure and fun for its own sake, your preference for predictability or spontaneity, and even your sensuality. Certain things that might entertain you in one context may irritate you in another—like playing video games during a wedding ceremony or listening to heavy metal music in a yoga class.

The next few quizzes are geared toward helping you and your partner deepen your understanding of one another's preferences in the realm of entertainment.

Quiz 1: Screens and Such

1. Your partner would describe their relationship to screens as:
    a. Ambivalent (Can't live with 'em, can't live without 'em.)
    b. Indifferent (Screens are just another tool.)
    c. Close (Screens are important.)
    d. Hooked (Screens are a lifeline.)

2. **(True/False)** The Internet connects people far more than it distances them.

3. Circle two words/phrases your partner associates with social media:

Fun	Entertaining
Business	Sad
Exciting	Overwhelming
Lonely	Bad
Confusing	Repellant
Time suck	Creativity
Risky	Boundaryless
Essential	Depressing
Wild, wild West	Good
Scary	Fascinating

4. **(True/False)** Your partner finds robots entertaining.

5. Your partner spends most of their screen time:
   a. Reading news
   b. Working
   c. Watching videos/movies
   d. Looking up recipes
   e. Shopping
   f. Checking the weather
   g. Conversing on Zoom or FaceTime

6. **(True/False)** Your partner listens to audiobooks and/or podcasts. (+1 bonus point if you can name one they're currently listening to.)

7. You could bribe your partner to forgo the Internet for one day with:
   a. $100
   b. A party
   c. A foot rub
   d. A séance

8. Your partner takes approximately ___ selfies a week.

9. Your partner's favorite TV or online streaming series is _____.

10. The movie your partner never gets tired of is _____.

PARTNER A TOTAL: _____

Quiz 1: Screens and Such

1. Your partner would describe their relationship to screens as:
   a. Ambivalent (Can't live with 'em, can't live without 'em.)
   b. Indifferent (Screens are just another tool.)
   c. Close (Screens are important.)
   d. Hooked (Screens are a lifeline.)

2. **(True/False)** The Internet connects people far more than it distances them.

3. Circle two words/phrases your partner associates with social media:

   Fun   Entertaining
   Business   Sad
   Exciting   Overwhelming
   Lonely   Bad
   Confusing   Repellant
   Time suck   Creativity
   Risky   Boundaryless
   Essential   Depressing
   Wild, wild West   Good
   Scary   Fascinating

4. **(True/False)** Your partner finds robots entertaining.

5. Your partner spends most of their screen time:
   a. Reading news
   b. Working
   c. Watching videos/movies
   d. Looking up recipes
   e. Shopping
   f. Checking the weather
   g. Conversing on Zoom or FaceTime

6. **(True/False)** Your partner listens to audiobooks and/or podcasts. (+1 bonus point if you can name one they're currently listening to.)

7. You could bribe your partner to forgo the Internet for one day with:
   a. $100
   b. A party
   c. A foot rub
   d. A séance

8. Your partner takes approximately ___ selfies a week.

9. Your partner's favorite TV or online streaming series is _____.

10. The movie your partner never gets tired of is _____.

PARTNER B TOTAL: _____

Quiz 2: Live and In Person

1. Your partner has *never* been to which type of event:
   a. Theater
   b. Musical concert
   c. Ballet
   d. Football game
   e. Competitive dog show

2. **(True/False)** Your partner is (or would be) a natural at charades.

3. If your partner entered a talent show, which talent of theirs would win it?
   a. Storytelling
   b. Music/singing
   c. Card tricks
   d. Dance
   e. Comedic skills

4. Where on this scale would your partner's competitiveness fall?

1	2	3	4	5
Very	Moderately	A little	Not really	Not at all

5. Your partner would definitely beat you at a game of:
   a. Foosball
   b. Tic-tac-toe
   c. Pinball
   d. Basketball
   e. *Pac-Man*
   f. Scrabble

6. **(True/False)** At an amusement park, your partner would ride roller coasters.

7. One entertainer your partner admires is

   _____.

8. The clothing item your partner is most likely to throw at their rock star crush is a:
   a. Sock
   b. T-shirt
   c. Bra
   d. Pair of boxer shorts

9. At a karaoke contest, your partner would probably win if they sang _____.

10. As a child, your partner most likely requested a balloon artist to make a:
   a. Sword
   b. Helmet
   c. Dog
   d. Heart
   e. Flower
   f. Crown

PARTNER A TOTAL: _____

Quiz 2: Live and In Person

1. Your partner has *never* been to which type of event:
    a. Theater
    b. Musical concert
    c. Ballet
    d. Football game
    e. Competitive dog show

2. **(True/False)** Your partner is (or would be) a natural at charades.

3. If your partner entered a talent show, which talent of theirs would win it?
    a. Storytelling
    b. Music/singing
    c. Card tricks
    d. Dance
    e. Comedic skills

4. Where on this scale would your partner's competitiveness fall?

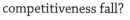

1	2	3	4	5
Very	Moderately	A little	Not really	Not at all

5. Your partner would definitely beat you at a game of:
    a. Foosball
    b. Tic-tac-toe
    c. Pinball
    d. Basketball
    e. *Pac-Man*
    f. Scrabble

6. **(True/False)** At an amusement park, your partner would ride roller coasters.

7. One entertainer your partner admires is

   _____.

8. The clothing item your partner is most likely to throw at their rock star crush is a:
   a. Sock
   b. T-shirt
   c. Bra
   d. Pair of boxer shorts

9. At a karaoke contest, your partner would probably win if they sang _____.

10. As a child, your partner most likely requested a balloon artist to make a:
   a. Sword
   b. Helmet
   c. Dog
   d. Heart
   e. Flower
   f. Crown

PARTNER B TOTAL: _____

REPLAY

This chapter's quizzes have pointed you toward new ways of thinking about games, shows, and events your partner finds entertaining. Hopefully, you've also learned more about the role of digital devices in your partner's life and how they may (or may not) help them unwind. Knowing what engages your partner will help you create more opportunities for sharing and uncovering new forms of entertainment together.

YOU'VE EARNED IT!

Quiz Master Prize: The Quiz Master chooses one of these three options:

1. Attend the event marked in question 1 of quiz 2 that you haven't yet experienced—theater, musical concert, ballet, football game, or competitive dog show.
2. Play the game your partner believes you'd win in question 5 of quiz 2 and see who *actually* wins.
3. Compete in a karaoke contest (even if it's in your own living room).

CHAPTER FIVE

Personalities

Although personality testing is a relatively new phe-nomenon (having come into vogue in the last hundred years), human beings have long tried to make sense of themselves, their reactions, and their temperaments by com-paring and contrasting different personality types. Whether through astrological signs, bumps on skulls, "four humors," or inkblots, every historical epoch has brought with it new frameworks for attempting to understand and predict people's tendencies, traits, and responses to their environment.

Nowadays, personality tests such as the Myers-Briggs Type Indicator (MBTI), the DISC assessment, the Enneagram, and the 16 PF Questionnaire are used for psychological diagnosis, employment screenings, and even just to satisfy our own curiosity about ourselves.

In this chapter's quizzes, we'll be considering personality mostly through the lens of the Big Five personality traits (five core traits that drive our behavior): openness, conscientious-ness, extraversion, agreeableness, and neuroticism.

Quiz 1: General Attitudes

1. Your partner's attitude improves by ___ percent within ___ minutes of _____.

2. Your partner's political beliefs are best described as:
   a. Liberal
   b. Centrist
   c. Conservative
   d. Libertarian
   e. Populist
   f. Anarchist

3. **(True/False)** A surprise birthday or anniversary party would delight your partner.

4. Your partner's attitude toward life is best described as:
   a. Glass half empty
   b. Glass half full
   c. Glass three-quarters full
   d. Don't even *think* about my glass!

5. If your partner were asked to close their eyes and fall backward into the arms of several strong acquaintances, where would you locate their trust level on this scale?

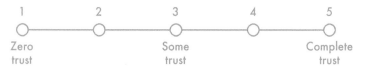

| 1 | 2 | 3 | 4 | 5 |
| Zero trust | | Some trust | | Complete trust |

6. Which sequence best describes your partner's default approach to life events?
   a. Feels, thinks, acts
   b. Thinks, feels, acts
   c. Acts, thinks, feels
   d. Thinks, acts, feels
   e. Acts, feels, thinks

7. **(True/False)** Your partner relaxes best in an orderly environment.

8. Of the five senses, the one your partner relies on most for pleasure is:
   a. Taste
   b. Touch
   c. Smell
   d. Sound
   e. Sight

9. **(True/False)** Stress motivates your partner to do their best work.

10. The word that encapsulates your partner's guiding principle in life is:
   a. Freedom
   b. Love
   c. Happiness
   d. Success
   e. Responsibility
   f. Fun
   g. Serving others
   h. Connection

PARTNER A TOTAL: _____

Quiz 1: General Attitudes

1. Your partner's attitude improves by ___ percent within ___ minutes of _____.

2. Your partner's political beliefs are best described as:
    a. Liberal
    b. Centrist
    c. Conservative
    d. Libertarian
    e. Populist
    f. Anarchist

3. **(True/False)** A surprise birthday or anniversary party would delight your partner.

4. Your partner's attitude toward life is best described as:
    a. Glass half empty
    b. Glass half full
    c. Glass three-quarters full
    d. Don't even *think* about my glass!

5. If your partner were asked to close their eyes and fall backward into the arms of several strong acquaintances, where would you locate their trust level on this scale?

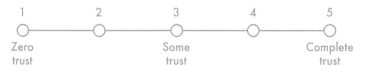

6. Which sequence best describes your partner's default approach to life events?
   a. Feels, thinks, acts
   b. Thinks, feels, acts
   c. Acts, thinks, feels
   d. Thinks, acts, feels
   e. Acts, feels, thinks

7. **(True/False)** Your partner relaxes best in an orderly environment.

8. Of the five senses, the one your partner relies on most for pleasure is:
   a. Taste
   b. Touch
   c. Smell
   d. Sound
   e. Sight

9. **(True/False)** Stress motivates your partner to do their best work.

10. The word that encapsulates your partner's guiding principle in life is:
    a. Freedom
    b. Love
    c. Happiness
    d. Success
    e. Responsibility
    f. Fun
    g. Serving others
    h. Connection

PARTNER B TOTAL: _____

Quiz 2: You with Others

1. One statement that sums up your partner's attitude toward humanity is _____ _____.

2. **(True/False)** People tend to find your partner "warm and friendly."

3. Socially, your partner prefers to hang out with:
    a. You and one other couple
    b. You in a large group of people
    c. You in a small group of people
    d. Just the two of you

4. **(Circle one.)** Your partner wants **more adventure** / **more peace** in their life.

5. Your partner sees themself as:
    a. Extroverted
    b. Mostly extroverted
    c. Introverted
    d. Mostly introverted
    e. An ambivert, or a mix of both extroverted and introverted

6. **(True/False)** Your partner will say yes to out-of-the-box ideas.

7. If someone crosses a line in conversation, your partner:
   a. Removes themself
   b. Confronts the speaker
   c. Changes the subject
   d. Uses humor to deflect

8. **(Circle one.)** Your partner tends to be **guarded** / **open** with new people.

9. In one sentence, describe a cringe-worthy experience your partner has had in public: _____
   _____.

10. To reach a goal, your partner relies on:
    a. Self-discipline
    b. A coach
    c. Stress-free time
    d. Deadlines
    e. Caffeine

    PARTNER A TOTAL: _____

Quiz 2: You with Others

1. One statement that sums up your partner's attitude toward humanity is _____
_____.

2. **(True/False)** People tend to find your partner "warm and friendly."

3. Socially, your partner prefers to hang out with:
   a. You and one other couple
   b. You in a large group of people
   c. You in a small group of people
   d. Just the two of you

4. **(Circle one.)** Your partner wants **more adventure / more peace** in their life.

5. Your partner sees themself as:
   a. Extroverted
   b. Mostly extroverted
   c. Introverted
   d. Mostly introverted
   e. An ambivert, or a mix of both extroverted and introverted

6. **(True/False)** Your partner will say yes to out-of-the-box ideas.

7. If someone crosses a line in conversation, your partner:
    a. Removes themself
    b. Confronts the speaker
    c. Changes the subject
    d. Uses humor to deflect

8. **(Circle one.)** Your partner tends to be **guarded** / **open** with new people.

9. In one sentence, describe a cringe-worthy experience your partner has had in public: _____
_____.

10. To reach a goal, your partner relies on:
    a. Self-discipline
    b. A coach
    c. Stress-free time
    d. Deadlines
    e. Caffeine

PARTNER B TOTAL: _____

Quiz 3: Just You

1. Your partner likes it when you allow them to:
   a. Take the lead often
   b. Take the lead sometimes
   c. Share leadership equally
   d. Follow your lead

2. A personality trait your partner hopes to elicit from you more often is your _____.

3. Your partner is most talkative during the:
   a. Morning
   b. Afternoon
   c. Evening
   d. Night

4. **(True/False)** Your partner believes "a good, clean fight" can bring you closer.

5. When your partner feels sad, what you do that helps them snap out of it is:
   a. Make jokes
   b. Offer a hug
   c. Talk them through it
   d. Be present and loving
   e. Invite them to do something active

6. **(True/False)** Your partner believes it's more important to relax than push limits.

7. Your partner has felt happiest with you while:
   a. Touching
   b. Talking
   c. Sitting in silence
   d. Doing a fun activity together

8. **(True/False)** Your partner occasionally includes astrological analysis in their decisions.

9. One thing your partner can't stand seeing in a bathroom is _____.

10. Your partner secretly wants you to:
    a. Read to them
    b. Spoon them in the middle of the night
    c. Buy them a special gift
    d. Bake them cookies
    e. Write them a love poem

♥ A

PARTNER A TOTAL: _____

Quiz 3: Just You

1. Your partner likes it when you allow them to:
   a. Take the lead often
   b. Take the lead sometimes
   c. Share leadership equally
   d. Follow your lead

2. A personality trait your partner hopes to elicit from you more often is your _____.

3. Your partner is most talkative during the:
   a. Morning
   b. Afternoon
   c. Evening
   d. Night

4. **(True/False)** Your partner believes "a good, clean fight" can bring you closer.

5. When your partner feels sad, what you do that helps them snap out of it is:
   a. Make jokes
   b. Offer a hug
   c. Talk them through it
   d. Be present and loving
   e. Invite them to do something active

6. **(True/False)** Your partner believes it's more important to relax than push limits.

7. Your partner has felt happiest with you while:
   a. Touching
   b. Talking
   c. Sitting in silence
   d. Doing a fun activity together

8. **(True/False)** Your partner occasionally includes astrological analysis in their decisions.

9. One thing your partner can't stand seeing in a bathroom is
   _____.

10. Your partner secretly wants you to:
    a. Read to them
    b. Spoon them in the middle of the night
    c. Buy them a special gift
    d. Bake them cookies
    e. Write them a love poem

PARTNER B TOTAL: _____

REPLAY

You've gotten into some of the nooks and crannies of one another's personalities in this chapter, comparing and contrasting your life philosophies. You've also considered one another's temperaments and tendencies through questions that touch on the Big Five personality traits of openness, conscientiousness, level of extraversion, agreeableness, and neuroticism.

YOU'VE EARNED IT!

Quiz Master Prize: The Quiz Master is entitled to ask their partner to arrange an outing that fits the "social event" criteria of their selection in question 3 of quiz 2. For example, "Can you organize a night out tomorrow with our friends?" or "Can you get us tickets to an open-air banjo concert in the next few days?"

CHAPTER SIX

Friends and Family

My Spanish-born father used to warn me: *Dime con quién andas y te diré quién eres* ("Tell me who you walk with, and I'll tell you who you are"). It was his way of trying to discourage me from spending time with friends he thought were a bad influence—a category *all* my friends seemed to fit into during my teenage years. Although I still wish he'd valued my friends from that time more than he did, I can appreciate the seed of wisdom in this Spanish truism. The people we "walk with" do rub off on us, as we do on them.

The same holds true for family. Whether you're from a tightly knit family that collapses into a puppy pile at holiday events or from a family that rarely communicates their feelings, all of us have been shaped by relationships with family members and friends.

In these quizzes, you'll look more closely at who you and your partner "walk with."

Quiz 1: We Are Family

1. A family tradition your partner would like to keep alive is

   _____.

2. **(True/False)** Your partner believes loyalty to family involves self-sacrifice.

3. An alternate name your partner might have liked to have been given at birth is _____.

4. One positive thing you do that reminds your partner of their favorite parent is _____.

5. What is a yearly family holiday event your partner prefers to avoid?
   a. Hanukkah/Christmas/Kwanzaa
   b. Ramadan
   c. Thanksgiving
   d. New Year's Eve
   e. Mother's Day
   f. Father's Day
   g. Halloween

6. **(Circle one.)** Your partner **loves** / **loathes** the mom, dad, kid, dog, and cat stickers on the rear windows of cars representing the driver's family constellation.

7. How frequently does your partner communicate (including texting, videoconferencing, IMing, and e-mailing) with their close relative(s)?

    a. Hourly

    b. Daily

    c. Weekly

    d. Monthly

    e. Yearly

8. The relative your partner most resembles is

    _____.

9. Your partner thinks the ideal size for a nuclear family is:

    a. Two

    b. Three

    c. Four

    d. Five

    e. Six

    f. Seven or more

10. **(True/False)** Family members regularly show up in your partner's nighttime dreams.

    PARTNER A TOTAL: _____

Quiz 1: We Are Family

1. A family tradition your partner would like to keep alive is
    _____.

2. **(True/False)** Your partner believes loyalty to family involves self-sacrifice.

3. An alternate name your partner might have liked to have been given at birth is _____.

4. One positive thing you do that reminds your partner of their favorite parent is _____.

5. What is a yearly family holiday event your partner prefers to avoid?
    a. Hanukkah/Christmas/Kwanzaa
    b. Ramadan
    c. Thanksgiving
    d. New Year's Eve
    e. Mother's Day
    f. Father's Day
    g. Halloween

6. **(Circle one.)** Your partner **loves** / **loathes** the mom, dad, kid, dog, and cat stickers on the rear windows of cars representing the driver's family constellation.

7. How frequently does your partner communicate (including texting, videoconferencing, IMing, and e-mailing) with their close relative(s)?
   a. Hourly
   b. Daily
   c. Weekly
   d. Monthly
   e. Yearly

8. The relative your partner most resembles is

   _____.

9. Your partner thinks the ideal size for a nuclear family is:
   a. Two
   b. Three
   c. Four
   d. Five
   e. Six
   f. Seven or more

10. **(True/False)** Family members regularly show up in your partner's nighttime dreams.

   PARTNER B TOTAL: _____

Quiz 2: Keep Your Friends Close

1. The first name of your partner's best friend in elementary school was _____.

2. **(True/False)** Your partner believes friendships can threaten close romantic relationships.

3. The wackiest situation your partner was ever roped into by a friend involved:
    a. Tarot cards
    b. Cursing parrots
    c. Jell-O
    d. Running out of gasoline
    e. Crashing a wedding
    f. Dressing up as an elf
    g. Other: _____

4. **(Circle one.)** When things "go wrong," what your partner needs most from a friend is **loving attention** / **practical advice**.

5. **(Circle one.)** Your partner has more **historical friendships** / **more recent friendships**.

6. Where did your partner meet the majority of their current friends?
    a. Neighborhood
    b. Religious/spiritual community

c.   High school

d.   College/graduate school

e.   Office

f.   Other: _____

7.   What's the total number of your partner's closest friends?

a.   One to three

b.   Four to six

c.   Seven to nine

d.   10 or more

8.   List an object a close friend once gave your partner that they treasure: _____.

9.   One thing your partner used to do with friends in high school to cope, get attention, or find fulfillment is:

a.   Break rules

b.   Run for school council

c.   Test limits

d.   Make art

e.   Use mind-altering substances

f.   Play in a band

g.   Play sports

h.   Design the yearbook or school newspaper

i.   Other: _____

10. Your partner's first cake-and-balloons birthday party took place at age ____.

PARTNER A TOTAL: _____

Quiz 2: Keep Your Friends Close

1. The first name of your partner's best friend in elementary school was _____.

2. **(True/False)** Your partner believes friendships can threaten close romantic relationships.

3. The wackiest situation your partner was ever roped into by a friend involved:
   a. Tarot cards
   b. Cursing parrots
   c. Jell-O
   d. Running out of gasoline
   e. Crashing a wedding
   f. Dressing up as an elf
   g. Other: _____

4. **(Circle one.)** When things "go wrong," what your partner needs most from a friend is **loving attention** / **practical advice**.

5. **(Circle one.)** Your partner has more **historical friendships** / **more recent friendships**.

6. Where did your partner meet the majority of their current friends?
   a. Neighborhood
   b. Religious/spiritual community

    c.   High school

    d.   College/graduate school

    e.   Office

    f.   Other: _____

7. What's the total number of your partner's closest friends?

    a.   One to three

    b.   Four to six

    c.   Seven to nine

    d.   10 or more

8. List an object a close friend once gave your partner that they treasure: _____.

9. One thing your partner used to do with friends in high school to cope, get attention, or find fulfillment is:

    a.   Break rules

    b.   Run for school council

    c.   Test limits

    d.   Make art

    e.   Use mind-altering substances

    f.   Play in a band

    g.   Play sports

    h.   Design the yearbook or school newspaper

    i.   Other: _____

10. Your partner's first cake-and-balloons birthday party took place at age ____.

PARTNER B TOTAL: _____

REPLAY

You've just completed a few quizzes geared at revealing what you know—and what you're still learning—about your partner's most significant interpersonal relationships. Now's a good time to reflect on the new information you've unearthed and how your understanding of your partner's friendships and family relationships has deepened.

YOU'VE EARNED IT!

Quiz Master Prize: Arrange a get-together at a park, in your home, or at a coffee shop with one or more of the Quiz Master's friends, depending on their preference. Be sure to find out from them what would make this event fun and pleasurable.

CHAPTER SEVEN
Travel

In order to grow and thrive, each of us balances two critical needs: the need for security and the need for autonomy. As children, for healthy development, we require what psychologists refer to as a "secure base" in our relationship with at least one caregiver, someone we can count on to be there for us when we need them. At the same time, we seek out novelty, incrementally testing the waters of our own independence, stepping out of our comfort zones, taking on challenges, and expanding our sense of mastery in the world.

As adults, traveling is one way to continue expanding. Whether we're going to a nearby town or halfway across the world, the impetus for big and small journeys has roots in our earliest developmental strivings. The desire to move beyond the limitations of our families, our neighborhoods, and our own culture helps us become who we truly are. In the words of philosopher and author Alain de Botton: "People only get really interesting when they start to rattle the bars of their cages."

In these quizzes, you'll be thinking more deeply about travel and what it means to both of you.

Quiz 1: Everyday Travels

1. When your partner daydreams about traveling, they mostly think about _____.

2. To make a long commute more pleasurable, your partner:
    a. Reads bumper stickers
    b. Drinks coffee
    c. Listens to a podcast
    d. Reads a book
    e. Enjoys the scenery
    f. Checks social media on their phone

3. **(True/False)** Your partner considers themself to be an easy, flexible traveling companion.

4. The last enjoyable stroll your partner took was:
    a. Around the block
    b. Through a park
    c. In a mall
    d. On a beach
    e. On a treadmill

5. Your partner's preferred method of travel is:
    a. Train/bus/metro
    b. Walking
    c. Ferry
    d. Bicycling
    e. Driving
    f. Riding a scooter
    g. Plane

6. A particular location inside or out that helps your partner feel peaceful is:
   a. A restaurant/diner
   b. A bench by a river/lake/ocean
   c. A café window
   d. A place in the woods
   e. A rooftop/fire escape

7. An interesting conversation your partner recently had with a stranger centered on:
   a. Weather
   b. Politics
   c. Philosophy
   d. Food
   e. Sports
   f. Music

8. In a guided visualization, to release stress, your partner would imagine themself:
   a. Lying in a hammock
   b. Listening to birds
   c. Smelling wildflowers
   d. Floating in water
   e. Other: _____

9. **(True/False)** Jack Kerouac's *On the Road* is one of your partner's favorite books.

10. A special place your partner frequented as a kid was

   _____.

   PARTNER A TOTAL: _____

Quiz 1: Everyday Travels

1. When your partner daydreams about traveling, they mostly think about _____.

2. To make a long commute more pleasurable, your partner:
   a. Reads bumper stickers
   b. Drinks coffee
   c. Listens to a podcast
   d. Reads a book
   e. Enjoys the scenery
   f. Checks social media on their phone

3. **(True/False)** Your partner considers themself to be an easy, flexible traveling companion.

4. The last enjoyable stroll your partner took was:
   a. Around the block
   b. Through a park
   c. In a mall
   d. On a beach
   e. On a treadmill

5. Your partner's preferred method of travel is:
   a. Train/bus/metro
   b. Walking
   c. Ferry
   d. Bicycling
   e. Driving
   f. Riding a scooter
   g. Plane

6. A particular location inside or out that helps your partner feel peaceful is:
   a. A restaurant/diner
   b. A bench by a river/lake/ocean
   c. A café window
   d. A place in the woods
   e. A rooftop/fire escape

7. An interesting conversation your partner recently had with a stranger centered on:
   a. Weather
   b. Politics
   c. Philosophy
   d. Food
   e. Sports
   f. Music

8. In a guided visualization, to release stress, your partner would imagine themself:
   a. Lying in a hammock
   b. Listening to birds
   c. Smelling wildflowers
   d. Floating in water
   e. Other: _____

9. **(True/False)** Jack Kerouac's *On the Road* is one of your partner's favorite books.

10. A special place your partner frequented as a kid was

    _____.

PARTNER B TOTAL: _____

Quiz 2: Oh, the Places I'll See

1. Your partner would most love to take you to which continent?
    a. Asia
    b. Africa
    c. North America
    d. South America
    e. Antarctica
    f. Europe
    g. Australia

2. One trip your partner took that changed their life was _____.

3. When traveling somewhere new and foreign, your partner likes to:
    a. Plan everything, soup to nuts
    b. Plan some things (e.g., book flights and hotels)
    c. Buy a one-way ticket and wing it
    d. Leave everything to chance

4. What three things would your partner want to have on a deserted island?

    _____

    _____

    _____

5. Your partner prefers to document their travels through:
    a. Journaling or writing
    b. Photographs
    c. E-mailing people or sharing on social media
    d. Drawings/sketches
    e. Just memory

6. The most uncommon food your partner has ever eaten in a faraway place was _____.

7. If they had one day in Rome, Istanbul, or Paris, your partner would:
    a. Get to know one historical landmark in detail
    b. Visit as many famous landmarks as possible
    c. Skip all landmarks and wander aimlessly
    d. Sit in a café or restaurant and observe people

8. **(Circle one.)** Your partner prefers the **window seat** / **aisle seat**.

9. If your partner took a two-week trip somewhere new, they'd bring:
    a. A backpack
    b. A carry-on suitcase
    c. A large suitcase and a carry-on
    d. Several suitcases and several carry-ons

10. The oddest thing that ever happened to your partner overseas (or somewhere new) was _____.

PARTNER A TOTAL: _____

Quiz 2: Oh, the Places I'll See

1. Your partner would most love to take you to which continent?
    a. Asia
    b. Africa
    c. North America
    d. South America
    e. Antarctica
    f. Europe
    g. Australia

2. One trip your partner took that changed their life was _____.

3. When traveling somewhere new and foreign, your partner likes to:
    a. Plan everything, soup to nuts
    b. Plan some things (e.g., book flights and hotels)
    c. Buy a one-way ticket and wing it
    d. Leave everything to chance

4. What three things would your partner want to have on a deserted island?

    _____
    _____
    _____

5. Your partner prefers to document their travels through:
   a. Journaling or writing
   b. Photographs
   c. E-mailing people or sharing on social media
   d. Drawings/sketches
   e. Just memory

6. The most uncommon food your partner has ever eaten in a faraway place was _____.

7. If they had one day in Rome, Istanbul, or Paris, your partner would:
   a. Get to know one historical landmark in detail
   b. Visit as many famous landmarks as possible
   c. Skip all landmarks and wander aimlessly
   d. Sit in a café or restaurant and observe people

8. **(Circle one.)** Your partner prefers the **window seat** / **aisle seat**.

9. If your partner took a two-week trip somewhere new, they'd bring:
   a. A backpack
   b. A carry-on suitcase
   c. A large suitcase and a carry-on
   d. Several suitcases and several carry-ons

10. The oddest thing that ever happened to your partner overseas (or somewhere new) was _____.

PARTNER B TOTAL: _____

REPLAY

Whether in towns, cities, states, provinces, or countries (or on other continents), in this chapter you've made some educated guesses about your partner's travels and their behaviors when journeying away from home. You've also likely discovered some of their daydreams and quirks as a traveler, from deserted island "must-haves" to the oddest thing that's happened to them overseas.

YOU'VE EARNED IT!

Quiz Master Prize: The Quiz Master chooses a "travel adventure" from these three options (or creates their own):

1. Invite your partner to your favorite local "relaxation" spot (question 6 of quiz 1).
2. Plan a trip together to the place you named in question 1 of quiz 2 (e.g., "Come with me to the Grand Canyon next month").
3. Lie on your living room floor while your partner leads you through a guided visualization based on your response to question 8 of quiz 1.

PART TWO

Us Together

In part 1, you and your partner worked separately, completed your copy of each quiz for points, and earned Quiz Master Prizes (or simply enjoyed the quizzes for their own sake). You'll be doing things a little differently in part 2. For the remainder of this book, you won't find the same quizzes repeated on separate pages. Now, you'll be taking them together and enjoying a more united couples quiz experience. To distinguish between your answers, I recommend you use different-colored markers and keep your colors consistent.

Remember those three-legged field day races in elementary school when you and your best friend tied your ankles together and stumbled over the grass toward the finish line? That's the idea here. You'll still be able to pass the book back and forth between you and calculate points; however, to "earn" a point, you and your partner simply need to participate and answer each question. There's no "correct" answer; points are given for initiative and follow-through. Work as a team, stay engaged, and cross the finish line together.

At the end of each chapter, you'll still find a suggested Quiz Master Prize in the "You've Earned It!" section; only now, this prize will be jointly won. If you prefer to come up with your own prize, do so. You always have the option of skipping this final section altogether. For some couples, simply taking the quizzes and learning more about each other is prize enough.

CHAPTER EIGHT
Best Qualities

It's not always easy to be authentic. Technology and social media feed into our self-doubt and insecurities, exerting pressure on many of us to present a "perfect" persona to a semi-imaginary audience of followers, friends, or professional colleagues. Constantly constructing and maintaining an attractive, successful, or happy facade can become a default setting in our approach to life. Sometimes, the only reliable psychic space where we feel free to relax and be ourselves is with our intimate partner.

In fact, the most important aspects of who we are need no enhancing, filtering, or editing. It's a relief to be able to trust that our partner will recognize our good qualities even when we fall short of our own or others' expectations, have a bad day, or reveal shortcomings.

Sometimes, although we're theoretically aware of our own best qualities, we're out of touch on a day-to-day level with what makes us special. In a partnership, we have a chance to see our best traits reflected in our partner's appreciation of us and to learn to value even those aspects of our partner's personality that appear to be radically different from our own.

Quiz 1: Seeing You at Your Best

1. What I consider to be *my* best quality:

   PARTNER A   PARTNER B

   _____   _____

2. What I consider to be *your* best quality:

   PARTNER A   PARTNER B

   _____   _____

3. Mark the top five qualities that keep a relationship sustainable.

loyalty	kindness	orderliness
trust	curiosity	boundaries
fidelity	understanding	cleanliness
self-control	respect	direct communication
courage	attentiveness	independence
self-compassion	listening	vulnerability
patience	empathy	humility

4. Go back and draw a star beside the one *most* important quality in the previous question.

5. **(True/False)** Nothing could be easier than being emotionally vulnerable.

6. When *I* recently embodied the best quality you listed in question 2:

   PARTNER A _____

   PARTNER B _____

7. In childhood, the person who modeled the trait I drew a star beside in question 3 was

    PARTNER A _____

    PARTNER B _____

8. **(True/False)** When it's true love, a relationship works like a well-oiled machine.

9. Mark one quality that's *not* crucial in a relationship.

loyalty	kindness	orderliness
trust	curiosity	strong convictions
fidelity	understanding	cleanliness
sense of humor	flexibility	empathy
self-control	respect	directness
courage	attentiveness	independence
self-compassion	listening	vulnerability
patience	stylishness	humility

10. The one important quality in a relationship we *both* need to work on is:
    a. Patience
    b. Self-compassion
    c. Vulnerability
    d. Honesty
    e. Other: _____

Quiz 2: What Others See in Us

1. A quality I think others see us bringing out in each other is:
   a. Positivity
   b. Open-mindedness
   c. Patience
   d. Kindness
   e. Other:

   _____

2. Three positive descriptors my caregiver(s) gave me as a child are:

   PARTNER A   **PARTNER B**

   _____   _____

   _____   _____

   _____   _____

3. One "set" of our complementary qualities that help us work together as a couple is:

   Flexible/structured   Cautious/generous

   Boundaried/compassionate   Blunt/diplomatic

   Other: _____

4. A quality I developed more *after* I was criticized for lacking it is:

   PARTNER A   **PARTNER B**

   _____   _____

5. Three compliments a teacher, boss, or authority figure has given me are:

   PARTNER A   **PARTNER B**

   _____   _____

   _____   _____

   _____   _____

6. **(True/False)** I'm good at translating seemingly critical comments into helpful feedback.

7. One hurtful message I received growing up was:
   a. You're not good enough
   b. You're too much
   c. You're too sensitive
   d. You're bad
   e. You're a burden
   f. Other: _____

8. What I did to try to prove that message wrong was:
   a. Became overly responsible
   b. Tried not to feel
   c. Tried to be perfect
   d. Became controlling
   e. Other: _____

9. A new, empowering message I can give myself is:
   a. You don't have to be perfect to be loved
   b. It's okay to make mistakes and learn
   c. Others value the real you
   d. You're not responsible for others
   e. It's okay to trust and let go
   f. Other: _____

10. My best self comes out most with you when I feel:

   PARTNER A   PARTNER B

   _____   _____

Quiz 3: Bringing Out the Best in Each Other

1. Circle three words that capture what first attracted us to each other.

Kindness	Charisma	Comfort
Positivity	Authenticity	Confidence
Attentiveness	Attractiveness	Thoughtfulness
Ambition	Seriousness	Respectfulness
Humor	Sociability	Integrity

2. What I noticed you do today that conveyed one of the qualities from question 1 is:

   PARTNER A   PARTNER B

   _____   _____

3. What helps me think most positively about us is:
   a. Spending time together
   b. Showing physical affection often
   c. Sharing thoughts and feelings
   d. Going on adventures
   e. Other: _____

4. **(True/False)** I tend to be most productive when I'm under pressure.

5. What would help me connect more with you after we've been away from each other is:
   a. 10 expectation-free minutes with you
   b. A long hug
   c. You looking me in the eye and saying, "I missed you"

d.   Casual chatting

e.   Other: _____

6. **(True/False)** We do better visiting our respective families when we plan how we're going to handle family dynamics in advance.

7. We compare ourselves to other couples:

a.   All the time

b.   A lot

c.   Sometimes

d.   Never

8. What most affects my ability to be at my best with you is:

a.   Lack of sleep

b.   Hunger

c.   Lack of connection

d.   Lack of space

e.   Stress

f.   Illness

9. One simple thing you say or do that helps me reset when I'm grumpy is:

PARTNER A   PARTNER B

_____   _____

10. Something we do together that seems to bring out the best in both of us is:

PARTNER A   PARTNER B

_____   _____

REPLAY

You've used this chapter to reflect on your best qualities. You've also touched on what, in your view, makes
a relationship sustainable. It hasn't all been rainbows
and unicorns either—you've recognized where each of
you needs to continue evolving to create more satisfac-
tion in your partnership and to become more of your
best selves.

YOU'VE EARNED IT!

Quiz Master Prize: Get a coin and decide who will be
heads and who will be tails. Flip the coin. Whoever's
side lands faceup gets to initiate the activity their partner listed as "what brings out the best in both of you"
in question 10 of quiz 3. For example, you might say,
"Let's go to the movies tomorrow night" or "Let's take
a nature walk in a half an hour."

CHAPTER NINE

Intimacy

Many couples talk about wanting intimacy. They sense when it's absent but struggle to recognize its presence. Couples who are together for decades sometimes complain of rarely experiencing it or of having radically different opinions about what generates or erodes it. *Is my partner capable of it? Am I capable of it?* The fact that intimacy can be used as a stand-in term for sex can further confuse and convolute its meaning. But sex isn't always intimate, and of course intimacy doesn't have to be sexual.

Intimacy isn't something *outside* us. It's a measure of our capacity to know another person in different ways and to be known ourselves—a dynamic interplay of qualities and emotional states such as curiosity, trust, courage, and receptivity.

I see intimacy as a relational superpower that quietly strengthens itself within us the more we get to know who we are, what we feel and think, and why—all in the context of our relationship to others and the world. The greater our capacity to know ourselves, the greater our capacity both to allow ourselves to be known and to get to know another person.

Quiz 1: Emotional Intimacy

1. **(True/False)** I believe intimacy and privacy are mutually exclusive.

2. I remember our first truly intimate moment occurring when:

   PARTNER A   PARTNER B

   _____   _____

3. **(Circle all that apply.)** The daily practice(s) I do to stay in touch with my feelings are:

   Meditation

   Reading thought-provoking books

   Walking/hiking/running

   Yoga

   Journaling

   Prayer

   Other: _____

4. My vulnerability comfort level with you on a scale from 1 to 5 is:

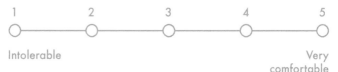

   Intolerable   Very comfortable

5. **(True/False)** I prefer being asked if I'm available to listen before you share something personal or emotionally charged.

6. The emotion I'm least comfortable with is:

   a. Helplessness   e. Anxiety

   b. Sadness   f. Loneliness

   c. Anger   g. Other:

   d. Guilt   _____

7. A fear that prevents me from opening up to you is:

   a. Fear of being too much

   b. Fear of not being enough

   c. Fear of judgment

   d. Fear of abandonment

   e. Other: _____

8. In what way, other than verbal, do I express my feelings to you?

   PARTNER A   PARTNER B

   _____   _____

9. **(Circle all that apply.)** I feel most emotionally intimate with you when:

   I see/feel/sense/hear how much you need me

   You show me your less "acceptable" emotions
   (fear, sadness, shame, anger, etc.)

   We spend time together with no distractions

   We work through disagreements together

   You listen to me empathically without trying to "fix" me

   Other: _____

10. Being close to you emotionally strengthens my:

    PARTNER A   PARTNER B

    _____   _____

Quiz 2: Physical Intimacy

1. A casual form of touch I enjoy receiving from you is:

    PARTNER A   **PARTNER B**

    _____   _____

2. After some form of sexual/sensual contact, what I like doing most is:
    a. Holding you/lying in your arms
    b. Being alone for a bit
    c. Chatting
    d. Other: _____

3. **(True/False)** Partners should intuitively know how to arouse each other.

4. The part of my body I yearn for you to touch more is:

    PARTNER A   **PARTNER B**

    _____   _____

5. The part of my body I suspect you yearn to touch more is:

    PARTNER A   **PARTNER B**

    _____   _____

6. A place I generally don't like to be touched is:
    a. Neck
    b. Arms
    c. Head
    d. Cheeks
    e. Other: _____

7. A difficult experience (illness, accident, etc.) that increased our intimacy was _____.

8. What might help me feel physically closer to you is:
   a. Holding hands
   b. Eye gazing
   c. More regular hugging
   d. Walking side by side (not in front or behind)
   e. Other: _____

9. One fun or silly sensual activity I'd like to try with you is:

   PARTNER A   **PARTNER B**

   _____ _____

10. **(True/False)** We could use more practice regularly touching each other.

Quiz 3: Intimacy in Action

1. Rate these possible Saturday-morning activities on a scale from 1 to 5 (where 1 = "not interested" and 5 = "very interested").

    PARTNER A ___, PARTNER B ___ Going for a walk/hike

    PARTNER A ___, PARTNER B ___ Shower or bath

    PARTNER A ___, PARTNER B ___ Cooking brunch

    PARTNER A ___, PARTNER B ___ Being sexual

    PARTNER A ___, PARTNER B ___ Socializing with friends

    PARTNER A ___, PARTNER B ___ Gardening

    PARTNER A ___, PARTNER B ___ Board game

2. One aspect of our sex life I really enjoy is:

    PARTNER A   PARTNER B

    _____   _____

3. One romantic action I've never experienced but might enjoy is:

    a. Receiving a love letter

    b. Taking a shower or bath together

    c. Making out in the back seat of a car

    d. Allowing you to shave my face/legs

    e. Other: _____

4. The "term of endearment" I most enjoy using with you is:

    PARTNER A   PARTNER B

    _____   _____

5. **(True/False)** You might try new things in bed if I risked asking for them.

6. If we were both in the mood to slow dance, the song you'd probably choose to dance to is:

_____   _____

7. One way I avoid intimacy with you is:
    a. I make assumptions rather than asking you
    b. I keep/get busy
    c. I flood you with my emotions
    d. I stuff my feelings down

8. During our downtime, what brings us closer is

_____.

9. An intimate statement I love hearing you say is:

PARTNER A _____

_____

PARTNER B _____

_____

10. In public, one way I'd like you to try to sustain our closeness would be to:
    a. Squeeze my hand
    b. Kiss me spontaneously
    c. Whisper, "I love you"
    d. Make eye contact and smile
    e. Other: _____

REPLAY

In this chapter, we've looked at some specifics related to what emotional and physical intimacy mean in your relationship. We've also identified actions, words, phrases, and activities you can draw on to foster more intimacy.

YOU'VE EARNED IT!

Quiz Master Prize: Look at the romantic action you both marked (in different-colored ink) for question 3 of quiz 3 in this chapter. Both of you spontaneously initiate this action for your partner within the next 12 to 24 hours (or within another mutually agreed-upon time frame). If your partner circled "receiving a love letter," you might write your partner a heartfelt love letter and slip it under their pillow or the windshield wiper of their car. If they selected "taking a shower or bath together," you might ask them if they'll take a shower with you before bed.

CHAPTER TEN
Our Past

Did you and your partner fall in love last week on a dating app? Or did you first kiss each other on prom night fifty years ago? Either way, there's one basic, fundamental fact that holds true across virtually all relationships, no matter how briefly or how long you've been a couple. Put simply: As long as you and your partner are together, you are with *another person.*

This may seem bewilderingly obvious to you. "Of course I'm with another person." But over the past 14 years of working with many different couples on getting the most out of their relationships, I can assure you that some of the biggest problems between romantic partners arise because they regularly and consistently "forget" that their partner isn't an extension of them. Every partner in every couple is 100 percent their own person . . . and has a right to be! This doesn't mean anyone should put up with hurtful or aggressive behavior; it simply means we get nowhere fast by imposing our way of being on another person as the "only" or "right" way.

Along with variations in temperament, attitude, personality, styles, and physical appearance, another important factor that shapes the differences between two people in a couple is their history. We'll be looking at some of the ways your past affected you and at how you're challenging one another to grow into greater wholeness now.

Quiz 1: How We Met

1. One memorable moment I still recall about the day we first met is:

   PARTNER A _____

   PARTNER B _____

2. Something I initially misjudged about you was:
   a. Your intellect
   b. Your sense of humor
   c. Your sense of style
   d. Your integrity
   e. Your generosity
   f. Other: _____

3. Our initial attraction to one another was mostly:
   a. Emotional
   b. Physical
   c. Intellectual
   d. Spiritual

4. If we could go back in time and relive our first meeting, one thing we might do differently is:

   PARTNER A _____

   PARTNER B _____

5. **(True/False)** We will both wait in long lines to see any new Star Wars movie.

6. **(Circle one.)** Looking back, I would rather have met you **a few months earlier** / **a few months later**.

7. If I could do our first date over again, I would:
    a. Be more vulnerable
    b. Kiss you sooner
    c. Be more spontaneous
    d. Tell you how attractive you are
    e. Ask you more questions and listen more closely
    f. Answer your questions more sincerely
    g. Other: _____

8. One of my quirks I believe you immediately found endearing was:

    PARTNER A _____

    PARTNER B _____

9. Who deserves more credit than we've given them for the fact that we met?
    a. A certain family member
    b. A certain friend
    c. A professional colleague
    d. An acquaintance
    e. A stranger
    f. Other: _____

10. What peculiar event contributed to us meeting?

    PARTNER A _____

    PARTNER B _____

Quiz 2: Our "Firsts"

1. What I liked about you instantly was:
   a. Your smile
   b. Your sense of humor
   c. Your smell
   d. Your passion
   e. Your goodness
   f. Your confidence
   g. Your attractiveness
   h. Your kindness
   i. Other: _____

2. **(Circle one.)** The first time I felt jealousy with you, **I kept it to myself / I shared it with you**.

3. During our first competitive game, I remember you:
   a. Going in for the kill
   b. Being "nice" and backing off
   c. Bending rules
   d. Outright cheating
   e. Other: _____

4. What I remember about the first moment I felt truly "seen" by you is:

   PARTNER A _____

   PARTNER B _____

5. **(Circle one.)** If we got trapped in the space-time continuum, I would rather **eternally relive our first romantic date / eternally relive our last satisfying sexual experience with one another**.

6. What did you like about my family the first time you met them?

   PARTNER A _____

   PARTNER B _____

7. One of the most memorable tender "firsts" we had was:
   a. Taking care of each other when one of us was sick
   b. Listening to you talk in your sleep
   c. Making up after a difficult fight
   d. The first time we shared how we felt about each other
   e. Other: _____

8. **(True/False)** I remember the first time you wiped tears off my face.

9. Match up two events with the locations (or write in your own to complete the matchup). (+1 bonus point if you can match up every item in the left-hand column.)

First kiss	Movie theater
First memorable apology	Street
First time meeting family	Restaurant
First meaningful gift	Your place
First use of term boy/girlfriend	My place

   _____   _____

   _____   _____

10. **(True/False)** I clearly remember the first time we laughed so hard we cried.

Quiz 3: What We've Learned

1. The most surprising thing I've learned about you since we met is:

   PARTNER A _____

   PARTNER B _____

2. Trying to control one another results in:
   a. Emotional distance
   b. Hurt feelings
   c. Self-judgment and blame
   d. Losing sight of one another's needs
   e. Other: _____

3. When I emotionally distance myself from you, you react by:

   PARTNER A _____

   PARTNER B _____

4. One practical thing I've learned from you is:
   a. How to get ketchup out of a bottle
   b. How to make a bed
   c. How to wrap a present
   d. Better money management skills
   e. Not to confuse dishwashing liquid with dishwasher detergent
   f. That personal hygiene is important
   g. To always keep a spare key
   h. Other: _____

5. The first time we deeply disappointed each other, it ended up helping us:
    a. Learn more about each other
    b. See past our projections
    c. Have more realistic expectations
    d. Recognize that we're two different people

6. **(True/False)** The one thing we'd both rush into a burning building to save is a beloved pet.

7. Our biggest challenge connecting as a couple is a result of:
    a. Poor work-life boundaries
    b. Overlooking what's good in ourselves and in our relationship
    c. Conflict avoidance
    d. Poor communication and misunderstandings
    e. Other: _____

8. The strangest accessory, piece of jewelry, or article of clothing I've ever seen you wear is:

    PARTNER A _____

    PARTNER B _____

9. **(True/False)** We have a relatively equal balance of power in our relationship.

10. I believe your most fundamental need is:
    a. To be cherished   d. To be protected
    b. To be heard   e. To be free
    c. To be respected   f. To play

REPLAY

In this chapter, you've revisited how you met and some
of your most important firsts. Recalling sweet, funny,
or tender details from important early moments of
your relationship can deepen your appreciation of one
another and what you've built together.

YOU'VE EARNED IT!

Quiz Master Prize: Look at your calendars and find
a time to return to the location of one of your most
memorable "firsts." Maybe it's a movie theater, a
restaurant, a diner, a lodge, a subway platform, or a
grocery store aisle. Once you agree on where you're
going, look at your answers for question 7 of quiz 1,
and put the behaviors you identified as what you
wished you'd both risked doing back then into action.

CHAPTER ELEVEN

Our Present

In *The Power of Now*, Eckhart Tolle writes: "The more you are focused on time—past and future—the more you miss the Now, the most precious thing there is." Your "now" as a couple is the present: both of you as you are, the world around you as it is. This doesn't mean you can't take stock of what needs to change and work on things you don't like (quiz 3 in this chapter, for example, focuses on growth opportunities in your relationship). Taking time to honor your present simply means you make a conscious effort to slow down and experience your life.

Spiritual enlightenment certainly doesn't have to be at the top of your to-do list as you work through these quizzes (though it could be, if you like). But acknowledging who you are, your complementarities, and the things you love about your relationship has benefits that can accrue and increase over time. When you bring awareness to the moment-to-moment experience of being human, it can release tension created in your body from too much habitual regretting or striving, helping you metabolize the good things life is already offering you.

Quiz 1: We Go Together Like . . .

1. Our differences are most complementary in the following area:

   a. Politics
   b. Sexuality
   c. Our social life
   d. Professionally
   e. Our personalities
   f. Finances

2. The idiomatic expression that most applies to us is:

   a. Opposites attract
   b. Birds of a feather flock together
   c. Soul mates
   d. Like oil and water
   e. Love at first sight
   f. Match made in heaven
   g. Joined at the hip

3. **(True/False)** We tend to counterbalance each other's reactions in stressful situations.

4. The positive qualities I deny in me but see in you are:

Humor	Competence	Determination
Irreverence	Intelligence	Know-how
Optimism	Sociability	Trust
Hopefulness	Charisma	Grit
Openness	Talent	Purposefulness
Strength	Generosity	Courage

5. One example of a time I embodied one of these qualities recently is:

    PARTNER A _____

    PARTNER B _____

6. The items we sometimes share include:

Car	Scooter	Credit card
Toothbrush	Blanket	Closet
Toothpaste	Socks	Hangers
Bed	Couch	Dresser
Belt	Computer	Jacket
Razor	Cup	Drawer
Bike	Refrigerator	

7. **(Circle all that apply.)** Which of these things do you do mostly because I don't want to?

    Drive you places   Assemble furniture

    Get rid of insects   Get groceries

    Take care of taxes   Other:

    Arrange social calendar   _____

    Calculate tips

8. The "seasonal pairing" that best describes us as a couple is:

    a. Summer/fall

    b. Fall/spring

    c. Spring/summer

    d. Winter/summer

    e. Winter/winter

    f. Other: _____

9. **(Check / add all that apply.)** The ingredients that go into creating the special cocktail representative of our relationship are:

	PARTNER A	PARTNER B
Seltzer	☐	☐
Cherry syrup	☐	☐
Lime juice	☐	☐
Salt	☐	☐
Sugar	☐	☐
Ice	☐	☐
Coffee liquer	☐	☐
Tequila	☐	☐
Rum	☐	☐
Vodka	☐	☐
Cola	☐	☐
Jalapeño pepper	☐	☐
Lemon peel	☐	☐
Mint	☐	☐
Fruit juice	☐	☐
Wine	☐	☐
_____	☐	☐
_____	☐	☐
_____	☐	☐

10. The name I would give this special "us" cocktail (such as the Cherry-Ice Fireball) is:

PARTNER A _____

PARTNER B _____

Quiz 2: Us Right Now

1. **(Circle one.)** Our connection rests mostly on a foundation of **integrity** / **interdependence**.

2. If we received an anonymous gift of 1,000 biodegradable, handmade pom-poms, something we might both enjoy doing with them is:
   a. Filling our tub with them and getting in naked together
   b. Throwing them off a roof and yelling, "It's raining pom-poms!"
   c. Placing them on people's windshields with the note "Pom-poms for Peace"
   d. Threading them onto a string to decorate our home
   e. Other: _____

3. **(True/False)** We are both excellent chimpanzee imitators.

4. What I think you enjoy most about your favorite season is:
   PARTNER A _____
   PARTNER B _____

5. What we're most proud of in our relationship is:
   a. How we listen to each other
   b. How we deal with differences
   c. How we make amends after fights
   d. How we work on our issues
   e. Other: _____

6. **(True/False)** Sometimes—even if only for a second or two—we allow ourselves to feel ridiculously, insanely grateful for each other.

7. One thing we have together I never dreamed I'd experience with another person is:
   a. Trust
   b. Love
   c. Safety
   d. Patience
   e. Well-being
   f. Sense of possibility
   g. Mutual respect
   h. Openness to change
   i. Other:
   _____

8. One thing I'll never have to regret on my deathbed since meeting you is:
   PARTNER A _____
   PARTNER B _____

9. What I wish we could do in slow motion so I could savor it more is:
   a. Kissing
   b. Hugging
   c. Intercourse
   d. Oral sex
   e. Hand holding
   f. Cuddling
   g. Eye gazing

10. One wonderful thing about our relationship we both take for granted is:
    PARTNER A _____
    PARTNER B _____

Quiz 3: Things to Improve Upon

1. One thing I could do to be a better partner to you is:

    PARTNER A _____

    PARTNER B _____

2. I look forward to the day we can reduce/give up:
    a. Complaining and negativity
    b. Alcohol and/or drug use
    c. Being defensive with one another
    d. Avoiding difficult conversations
    e. Mindless nutritional choices
    f. Other: _____

3. One language I've always wanted to learn is:

    PARTNER A _____

    PARTNER B _____

4. **(Circle all that apply.)** Less-than-classy bad habits that decrease the "romance" quotient in our relationship include:

    Throat clearing   Open gaseousness

    Genital scratching   Slouching

    Smoking   Cracking knuckles

    Nail biting   Public nail clipping

    Random cussing   Nose picking

    Infrequent bathing   Toothpicks in public

    Open-mouthed chewing   Pinky in ear

    Poor oral hygiene   Talking too loudly

5. One insecurity I could use support with is:
    a. Social skills
    b. Worthiness
    c. Self-doubt
    d. Attractiveness
    e. Intelligence
    f. Other: _____

6. The emotion that's hardest for us to deal with is:
    a. Anger
    b. Jealousy
    c. Helplessness
    d. Fear
    e. Disgust
    f. Sadness
    g. Joy

7. The one thing I've always resisted about becoming an "adult" is:
    PARTNER A _____
    PARTNER B _____

8. Something that might improve the way we handle money is:
    a. Having joint accounts
    b. Having separate accounts
    c. Once-weekly financial check-ins
    d. Talking to a financial advisor
    e. Other: _____

9. **(True/False)** When it comes to aspects of your personality I may not like (but can't change), I'm willing to practice acceptance and tolerance.

10. If I could do this one thing five times faster, my well-being level would skyrocket, positively affecting our relationship:

a. Driving to/from work
b. Getting ready in the morning
c. Winding down for bed
d. Working out
e. Answering e-mails
f. Cleaning up
g. Preparing meals

REPLAY

You've just spent time focusing on your complementarity as a couple in the here and now. You've also looked at aspects of your relationship that are pleasurable and positive. In this chapter's final quiz, you were invited to consider your personal flaws and insecurities— a necessary step if you want to make a good thing even better.

YOU'VE EARNED IT!

Quiz Master Prize: Look at the ingredients you checked or wrote down for the cocktail representation of your relationship in question 9 of quiz 1. Collect the ingredients you chose and work together as co-mixologists. Feel free to use a shaker if you have one. Test out different proportions as you refine your drink (serious kudos if you actually create something drinkable).

CHAPTER TWELVE
Our Future

In her book *Love Skills: The Keys to Unlocking Lasting, Wholehearted Love*, couples therapist Linda Carroll distills some of the most predictable emotional experiences of committed partnerships into five stages: The Merge, Doubt and Denial, Disillusionment, Decision, and Wholehearted Loving. In Carroll's view, love doesn't just fall into our laps with the right partner. We taste it in The Merge and then (seemingly) lose it over the course of the next several stages. At the Decision stage, we choose to move into Wholehearted Loving. But even the experience of wholehearted loving isn't a fixed, immutable state.

Keep this in mind as you work through the next three quizzes. When you and your partner discuss, plan, and daydream, try to envision a future that flexes and expands with who you both are, sharing your dreams as you might share the shifting landscapes in a kaleidoscope. Support one another in exploring what it means to make your own unique and evolving contribution to the world.

Carroll writes, "Living life, even from a place of wholeheartedness, is like walking through a labyrinth. You find detours, twists, and turns, and just when you think you're near the center, you come across another detour you didn't expect. Sometimes, though, when you think you are a long way from where you want to be, the obstacles disappear, and you are there."

Quiz 1: Our Partnership

1. In the future, a change I see for us in the way we handle money is:

   PARTNER A _____

   PARTNER B _____

2. What would make our political discussions more constructive is:
   a. Having more of them
   b. Having fewer of them
   c. Listening without interrupting
   d. Finding points of agreement/connection
   e. Wearing Halloween masks of the politicians we support

3. **(Circle one.)** In the future, I see us ***doing* more things together** / **just *being* more together**.

4. **(True/False)** People have mistaken us for siblings on occasion.

5. One new birthday, anniversary, or holiday tradition I'd like to adopt is:
   a. Reciprocal face painting
   b. Writing a new happy memory on a blackboard daily for a week
   c. Creating a treasure hunt at home
   d. Filling a donation jar all year long and then donating the funds to a local charity

e. Picking a wall in our house to decorate with "gratitude" sticky notes

f. Traveling somewhere we've never been

g. Making a simple three-question video interview of each other to look back on

h. Other: _____

6. My future couples fantasies tend to be about:
    a. Having a home
    b. Having a family
    c. Going on vacations
    d. Enjoying lavish luxuries
    e. Doing more community service
    f. Saving the planet

7. **(True/False)** We could create a relationship "mission statement" in 10 minutes.

8. A time capsule to our future selves would contain a "reminder" photo of us in this act:
    PARTNER A _____
    PARTNER B _____

9. Our relationship motto could be:
    a. Love fearlessly
    b. Love imperfectly
    c. Love patiently
    d. Love more
    e. All of the above

10. **(Circle one.)** I prefer **traditional** / **nontraditional** wedding celebrations.

Quiz 2: Our Dreams

1. A childhood dream I still harbor is:

   PARTNER A _____

   PARTNER B _____

2. Dreams are important because:
   a. They reflect hope
   b. They help people grow
   c. They inspire change
   d. They give life meaning
   e. Other: _____

3. One of my childhood dreams related to love and relationships is:

   PARTNER A _____

   PARTNER B _____

4. **(True/False)** Unfulfilled dreams are too painful to think about.

5. **(Circle all that apply.)** If I let myself dream big, I might dream of:

   Going skydiving   Being a CEO

   Writing a book   Inventing a lifesaving device

   Learning a special dance Going back to school

   Running a sports team   Other: _____

6. One of my childhood dreams related to money is:

    PARTNER A _____

    PARTNER B _____

7. One dream we could accomplish now if we took a chance is:

    a. Being pet owners

    b. Starting a business

    c. Traveling the world on a shoestring budget

    d. Having a kid

    e. Creating artwork

    f. Furthering a cause we believe in

    g. Other: _____

8. Something new we could do related to our nighttime dreams is:

    a. Keeping a dream journal by the bed

    b. Telling each other our dreams in detail more often

    c. Reading more literature on dreams

    d. Sharing ideas about dream symbols, meanings, and feelings

9. Something I loved doing as a child that's connected to one of my current passions:

    PARTNER A _____

    PARTNER B _____

10. **(True/False)** We both enjoy the feeling of flying in our dreams.

Quiz 3: Our Contribution

1. One protest march I would like to attend in the future would be for:

   PARTNER A _____

   PARTNER B _____

2. A step we could take toward reducing our carbon footprint is:

   a. Recycling more

   b. Switching to a plant-based diet

   c. Volunteering for environmental advocacy groups

   d. Installing solar panels

   e. Using public transportation

   f. Other: _____

3. A way I'd like to contribute to creating a better world is:

   PARTNER A _____

   PARTNER B _____

4. **(Circle all that apply.)** One way I've seen you contributing to others' well-being is:

   Paying the toll of the driver behind you

   Donating clothes

   Giving up your seat on the subway/metro/bus

   Doing pro bono work

   Writing a helpful review of a service or book

   Complimenting a stranger's outfit

Offering your umbrella to someone else

Smiling at someone just because

Being kind to a customer service rep or telemarketer

5. If we could leave a "sandwich" legacy to the world, the sandwich we'd invent would be:

PARTNER A _____

PARTNER B _____

6. An advertising agency wants us to pose naked for a photo shoot to sell its product on a Times Square billboard. What product might we agree to do this for?

    a. A nontoxic coating that reduces food waste

    b. A clothing line composed of 99 percent recycled trash

    c. Glasses that help people with vision impairments

    d. Nondairy egg substitutes

    e. Other: _____

7. **(True/False)** We've discussed the pros and cons of becoming a living organ donor.

8. **(Underline all that apply.)** We're willing to learn about—and make adjustments to—our diet, how we dispose of waste, how we travel, and how we spend our money if it doesn't align with our values.

9. **(Circle all that apply.)** Things I might do to contribute to others' well-being in our neighborhood are:

Shoveling snow from a stranger's sidewalk

Raking someone's leaves

Setting up a free outdoor library

Picking up litter

Starting a seedling exchange

Checking in on an elderly neighbor

Other: _____

10. If I could donate $1,000,000 to one charitable cause of my choice, it would be:

PARTNER A _____

PARTNER B _____

REPLAY

You've just answered questions about your vision for the future, your big and small dreams, and ways you can support each another while making a contribution.

YOU'VE EARNED IT!

Quiz Master Prize: In question 7 of quiz 1, you and your partner selected as either true or false the following statement: "We could create a relationship 'mission statement' in 10 minutes." If you both said "true," set a timer for 10 minutes, get your pens ready, and start writing. If one or both of you said "false," then do the same thing, seeing if you can come up with a mission statement in 10 minutes anyway.

Your relationship mission statement should have three parts: your shared relationship vision, a shared relationship core value, and a statement of your shared ultimate relationship goal. For example, a mission statement I created with my husband using this formula is: *We grow together through love and accountability into our highest potential.* (Full disclosure: This took us 12 and a half minutes to brainstorm and write.)

CHAPTER THIRTEEN

Our Couples Bucket List

When I was training to be a couples therapist, I learned about "stretching." In the context of couples work, a "stretch" is an action or behavior couples engage in to push past their comfort zones and become more loving partners. Stretches require us to do something we previously thought of as too difficult or unnatural to try. When a partner stretches out of their comfort zone, it can result in two positive outcomes simultaneously: It supplies the other partner with something they've been asking for—more connection, more intimacy, more love, more excitement—and it helps the partner doing the stretching reclaim some part of themselves that was dismissed, denied, or simply untapped within them. Stretching helps couples self-actualize while achieving a more interdependent, sustainable relationship.

Creating a Couples Bucket List is a way of mapping out some of your action-oriented "future stretches." These are big and small activities—either a bit challenging or very challenging—that will help you grow as people and as partners. They're not easy to do (otherwise, you would have already done them), but the challenge they present can be overcome.

Couples Bucket List

Review the items in this list. Check the ordinary and extraordinary adventures you want to stretch into one day, and add them to your Couples Bucket List (in the first column for Partner A and the second column for Partner B).

	PARTNER A	PARTNER B
Visit every continent	☐	☐
Run a marathon	☐	☐
See each other's childhood homes	☐	☐
Ice-skate at Rockefeller Center	☐	☐
Get a couples massage on a beach	☐	☐
Reenact our first date	☐	☐
Throw a big party for our closest friends and family	☐	☐
Sleep outside under the stars	☐	☐
Visit each other's high school or college campuses	☐	☐
Go boating down the Colorado River	☐	☐
Take a private, after-hours tour of the Sistine Chapel	☐	☐
Attend the ballet, opera, or symphony in formal attire	☐	☐
See Mount Everest	☐	☐
Have great-grandchildren	☐	☐
See an eclipse	☐	☐
Make gingersnap cookies together	☐	☐
Parachute from a plane	☐	☐
Walk the Great Wall of China	☐	☐
Ride a scooter across an island	☐	☐
Go to Mardi Gras	☐	☐
See the Northern Lights	☐	☐
Walk across a glacier	☐	☐

	PARTNER A	PARTNER B
Take turns sticking our tongues in each other's ears	☐	☐
Go to the real Oktoberfest	☐	☐
Roller-skate in gold-spangled disco outfits	☐	☐
Ride a carousel while hugging	☐	☐
Share and enact a sexual fantasy* together	☐	☐
Skip through puddles in a rainstorm	☐	☐
Skinny-dip in the sea at midnight	☐	☐
Paint a mural	☐	☐
_____	☐	☐
_____	☐	☐

*safe, consensual, and legal

REPLAY

You've spent the last chapter starting to consider big and small adventures you can take together as a couple to "stretch" out of your comfort zones and grow. Some of these adventures, like making gingersnap cookies, are things you might be able to do now, while others, like walking the Great Wall of China, could take some planning.

YOU'VE EARNED IT!

Quiz Master Prize: Combine the items you *both* selected onto a single Couples Bucket List. Make two copies of this document and frame them. Hang your framed Couples Bucket Lists where both of you will see them daily.

Bonus: Ask Me Anything

At the beginning of this book, I invited you to jot down any thoughts or questions that arose about your partner as you completed these quizzes. If you did, reread what you've written. Could your musings be folded into more specific questions you still have about your partner? If you didn't take notes, set aside a few minutes to reflect, either alone or with your partner, on what you learned over the course of this book.

Ask yourself, "What else do I really want to know about you? About our relationship?" Then tune in to your own body and wait. Imagine you're tuning in to a radio signal that includes feelings, mental images, and physical sensations. Notice what arises within—physically, energetically, emotionally, or in the form of visual images—in response to the question you've asked (this is an abbreviated version of "Focusing," a powerful self-awareness technique created by Eugene Gendlin). Once you've gotten clarity on what this "what else" might be for you, it's time to begin creating a round of unique, quiz-style questions of your own.

STEP 1. Write down your open-ended, multiple-choice, or true/false questions. For guidance on structuring your questions, refer back to earlier examples in this book.

STEP 2. Vet your questions for barbs or hidden motives. You'll connect most successfully with your partner when your questions are free of agendas and projections.

For example, if your question is "What was the name of the best lover you've ever had?" get clear on why you want to know this. If your partner gives you an answer you don't want to hear, will it distance you? If a question is emerging from your own anxiety, try changing it to something that will help you learn more about your partner no matter what they respond. For example, "What is your primary emotion when I ask you questions about past sexual experiences? a) Defensive b) Happy c) Scared d) Turned on e) Other: _____ "

STEP 3. Prepare yourself to release any attachment to your partner's answer. Monitor your own feelings and judgments once they respond. Whatever questions you ask in a committed love relationship, the key to creating a fruitful exchange is being mindful of (and responsible for) your own feelings, needs, and fears.

STEP 4. Practice listening in a way that implicitly communicates approval and acceptance. Develop a back-and-forth listener-speaker style of communication in which both partners equitably share roles and "air time." Structuring communication can help you both listen and speak productively.

This may mean getting yourself into the right headspace before asking questions. By reminding yourself that your partner is a separate person, entitled to their own thoughts, dreams, feelings, preferences, and past experiences, you're creating a safe, neutral zone where they can share themself more honestly and authentically with you.

Setting the intention to listen with love and be mindful of your hidden motives goes a long way toward helping your partner share who they truly are.

STEP 5. Check in with your partner to see if they're emotionally available before blurting out your questions. You may want to come up with a specific time of the day and/or of the week that's your designated "Question Time" so you're both prepared and in the right mindset to quiz each other and create your own personal Quiz Master Challenges.

STEP 6. When your partner asks you a question, do your best to answer it honestly, sincerely, and with an open heart. If you're the questioner, avoid judging your partner's responses. Let the meaning and implications of their answers sink in. Be sure to thank each other for asking questions and after answering, too. Your curiosity about one another is a gift—a sign that you care. Your willingness to share and disclose is also a gift—an act of trust.

References

Carroll, Linda. *Love Skills: The Keys to Unlocking Lasting, Whole-hearted Love*. Novato, CA: New World Library, 2020.

de Botton, Alain. "Quotable Quote." Accessed December 15, 2019. http://www.goodreads.com/quotes/399785.

Gendlin, Eugene T. *Focusing*. New York: Bantam Books, 1978.

Gottman, John, and Nan Silver. *The Seven Principles for Making Marriage Work*, revised. New York: Harmony, 2015.

"The Newlywed Game." *Wikipedia: The Free Encyclopedia*. Accessed November 20, 2019, http://en.wikipedia.org/wiki /The_Newlywed_Game.

Tolle, Eckhart. *The Power of Now: A Guide to Spiritual Enlightenment*. Novato, CA: New World Library, 1997.

Acknowledgments

I'm grateful to all the couples I've worked with, for inviting me into their worlds; it takes courage, humility, and grit to step into a therapist's office or teleconference. The MAIT book group has offered me a special space to connect around good books and good ideas. Mary Ray, Barbara Adams, Gloria Mog, Susan Roistacher, Suzanna Hillegass, Benta Sims, and Cindy Stauffer—I appreciate you! I'm grateful to my peer supervision group—Dianne Modell, Amy Clay, Leslie Rogers, Kevin Ogle, Renee Doe, and Isabel Kirk—for coming together monthly to engage in theoretical debates, informational exchanges, and clinical discussions. Also to Natalya Lunde—your gentle, easy presence in my life helps me feel at home, even in the suburbs. Anne Lowrey, thank you for your oversight on this project. Constance Santisteban, your rigorous, nuanced feedback brought clarity to these questions. Donna Otmani, powerhouse coach—thank you for being by my side this past year.

About the Author

Alicia Muñoz, LPC, is a couples therapist based in Virginia and the author of *No More Fighting: 20 Minutes a Week to a Stronger Relationship* and *A Journal of Us*. Alicia shares her views on the power of committed love-partnerships on her blog as well as in print and online magazines like *Mindbodygreen* and *Psychotherapy Networker*. You can sign up for her newsletter with tips on how to keep your relationship hot and healthy at www.aliciamunoz.com and follow her on Instagram at @aliciamunozcouples.

CPSIA information can be obtained
at www.ICGtesting.com
Printed in the USA
JSHW021631041221
20951JS00005B/6